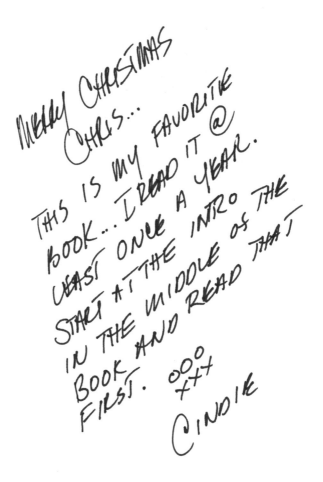

MERRY CHRISTMAS
CHRIS...
THIS IS MY FAVORITE
BOOK...I READ IT @
LEAST ONCE A YEAR.
START AT THE INTRO
IN THE MIDDLE OF THE
BOOK AND READ THAT
FIRST. ooo
xxx
CINDIE

RICK JOYNER
THE VISION

Two International Bestsellers
in One Volume

THE FINAL QUEST

THE CALL

THOMAS NELSON PUBLISHERS®
Nashville

Published in Nashville, Tennessee. Thomas Nelson is a trademark of Thomas Nelson, Inc.

The individual books in this omnibus edition were originally published in hardcover by MorningStar Publications, West U.S. Highway 421, Wilkesboro, NC 28697. *The Final Quest* Copyright © 1996, 1997, by Rick Joyner. *The Call* Copyright © 1999 by Rick Joyner.

Scripture quotations are taken from the NEW AMERICAN STANDARD BIBLE®, © Copyright The Lockman Foundation, 1960, 1962, 1963, 1968, 1971, 1972, 1973, 1975, 1977. Used by permission.

Library of Congress Cataloging-in-Publication Data

Joyner, Rick, 1949–
    The Vision : two international bestsellers in one volume / Rick Joyner.
        p. cm.

    ISBN 13: 978-0-7852-6713-3
    1. Armageddon. 2. End of the world. 3. Private revelations. I. Joyner, Rick, 1949–
Call. II. Title.
    BS649 .A68J68 2001
    248.2'9—dc21

Printed in the United States
12 QG 17 16

the Final Quest

Rick Joyner

MorningStar
PUBLICATIONS

The Final Quest

by Rick Joyner

First edition printed March 1996.

Second edition printed June 1996.

Hardcover edition printed June 1997.

Printed in the United States of America.

International Standard Book Number 1-878327-60-7.

To my wife,

Julie,

and our five children:

Anna, Aaryn, Amber, Ben and Sam.

May we all stand at the top of the mountain.

CONTENTS

Part I

the hordes of hell are marching

The demonic army was so large that it stretched as far as I could see. It was separated into divisions, with each carrying a different banner. The foremost divisions marched under the banners of Pride, Self-Righteousness, Respectability, Selfish Ambition, Unrighteous Judgment and Jealousy. There were many more of these evil divisions beyond my scope of vision, but those in the vanguard of this terrible horde from hell seemed to be the most powerful. The leader of this army was the Accuser of the Brethren himself.

The weapons carried by this horde were also named. The swords were named Intimidation; the spears were named Treachery; and the arrows were named Accusation, Gossip, Slander and Faultfinding. Scouts and smaller companies of demons—with such names as Rejection, Bitterness,

Impatience, Unforgiveness and Lust—were sent in advance of this army to prepare for the main attack.

These smaller companies and scouts were much fewer in number, but they were no less powerful than some of the larger divisions that followed. They were smaller only for strategic reasons. Just as John the Baptist was given an extraordinary anointing for baptizing the masses to prepare them for the Lord, these smaller demonic companies were given extraordinary evil powers for "baptizing the masses."

A single demon of Bitterness could sow his poison into multitudes of people, even entire races or cultures. A demon of Lust would attach himself to a single performer, movie or advertisement and send what appeared to be bolts of electric slime that would hit and "desensitize" great masses of people. All of this was to prepare for the great horde of evil which followed.

Although this army was marching specifically against the church, it also was attacking anyone else that it could. I knew that it was seeking to preempt a coming move of God, which was destined to sweep great numbers of people into the church.

The primary strategy of this army was to cause division on every possible level of relationship—churches with each other, congregations with their pastors, husbands and wives, children and parents, and even children with each other. The scouts were sent to locate the openings in churches, families or individuals that such spirits as Rejection, Bitterness and Lust could exploit and enlarge. Through these openings would pour demonic influences that completely overwhelmed their victims.

On the Backs of Christians

The most shocking part of this vision was that this horde was not riding on horses, but primarily on Christians! Most of them were well-dressed, respectable, and had the appearance of being refined and educated, but there also seemed to be representatives from almost every walk of life. While these people professed Christian truths in order to appease their consciences, they lived their lives in agreement with the powers of darkness. As they agreed with those powers, their assigned demons grew and more easily directed their actions.

Many of these believers were host to more than one demon, but one of the demons would clearly be in charge. The nature of the one in charge dictated which division it was marching in. Even though the divisions were all marching together, it also seemed that the entire army was on the verge of chaos. For example, the demons of Hate hated the other demons as much as they did the Christians. The demons of Jealousy were all jealous of one another.

The only way the leaders of this horde kept the demons from fighting each other was to keep their hatred focused on the people they were riding. However, these people would often break out in fights with each other. I knew that some of the armies that came against Israel in the Scriptures had ended up destroying themselves in this same way. When their purpose against Israel was thwarted, their rage was uncontrollable, and they began fighting each other.

I noted that the demons were riding *on* these Christians, but were not *in* them as was the case with non-Christians. It was obvious that these believers had only to stop agreeing with their demons in order to get free of them. For example, if the Christian on whom a demon of jealousy was riding just started to question the jealousy, that demon would weaken very fast. When this happened, the weakened demon would cry out and the leader of the division would direct all the demons around that Christian to attack him until the jealousy, etc., would build up on him again. If this did not work, the demons would begin quoting Scriptures, perverting them in a way that would justify the bitterness, accusations or other satanic influences they were spreading.

The power of the demons was clearly rooted almost entirely in the power of deception, but they had deceived these Christians to the point where they could use them and the Christians would think they were being used by God. This was because banners of Self-Righteousness were being carried by almost everyone, so that those marching could not even see the banners that marked the true nature of these divisions.

As I looked far to the rear of this army, I saw the entourage of the Accuser himself. I began to understand his strategy, and I was amazed that it was so simple. He knew that a house divided cannot stand, and his army represented an attempt to bring such division to the church that she would be powerless and ineffective.

It was apparent that the only way the Accuser could do this was to use Christians to war against their own brethren, and that is why almost everyone in the forward divisions was a Christian, or at least a professing Christian. Every step these deceived believers took in obedience to the Accuser strengthened his power over them. This made his confidence and the confidence of all his commanders grow with the progress of the army as it marched forward. It was apparent that the power of this army depended on the agreement of these Christians with the ways of evil.

15

The Prisoners

Trailing behind these first divisions was a multitude of other Christians who were prisoners of this army. All of these captive Christians were wounded, and they were guarded by smaller demons of Fear. There seemed to be more prisoners than there were demons in the army.

Surprisingly, these prisoners still had their swords and shields, but they did not use them. It was a shock to see that so many could be kept captive by so few of the little demons of Fear. If the Christians had just used their weapons, they could easily have freed themselves and probably done great damage to the entire evil horde. Instead, they marched submissively along.

Above the prisoners, the sky was black with vultures named Depression. Occasionally these would land on the shoulders of a prisoner and would vomit on him. The vomit was Condemnation. When the vomit hit a prisoner he would stand up and march a little straighter for a while, and then slump over, even weaker than before. Again, I wondered why the prisoners did not simply kill these vultures with their swords, which they could have easily done.

Occasionally the weaker prisoners would stumble and fall. As soon as they hit the ground, the other prisoners would begin stabbing them with their swords, scorning them for their weakness. The vultures would then come and begin devouring the fallen ones even before they were dead. The other Christian prisoners stood by and watched this approvingly, occasionally stabbing the fallen ones again with their swords.

As I watched, I realized that these prisoners thought the vomit of Condemnation was truth from God. Then I understood that these prisoners actually thought they were marching in the army of *God*! This is why they did not kill the little demons of fear or the vultures—they thought these were God's messengers! The darkness from the cloud of vultures made it so hard for these prisoners to see that they naively accepted everything that happened to them as being from the Lord. They felt that those who stumbled were under God's judgment, which is why they attacked them the way they did—they thought they were helping God!

The only food provided for these prisoners was the vomit from the vultures. Those who refused to eat it simply weakened until they fell. Those who did eat it were strengthened for a time, but with the strength of the evil one. Then they would weaken unless they would drink the waters of bitterness that were constantly being offered to them. After drinking the bitter waters, they would begin to vomit on the others. When one of the prisoners began to do this, a demon that was waiting for a ride would climb up on him and ride him up to one of the front divisions.

Satanic Slime

Even worse than the vomit from the vultures was a repulsive slime that these demons were urinating and defecating upon the Christians they rode. This slime was the pride, selfish ambition, etc., that was the nature of their division. However, this slime made the Christians feel so much better than the condemnation had, they easily believed that the demons were messengers of God. They actually thought this slime was the anointing of the Holy Spirit.

I had been so repulsed by the evil army that I wanted to die. Then the voice of the Lord came to me saying, *"This is the beginning of the enemy's last-day army. This is Satan's ultimate deception. His ultimate power of destruction is released when he uses Christians to attack one another. Throughout the ages he has used this army, but never has he been able to use so many for his evil purposes as he is now. Do not fear. I have an army too. You must now stand and fight, because there is no longer any place to hide from this war. You must fight for My kingdom, for truth, and for those who have been deceived."*

This word from the Lord was so encouraging that I immediately began yelling to the Christian prisoners that they were deceived, thinking that they would listen to me. When I did this, it seemed that the whole army turned to look at me. The cloud of fear and depression that was over them started to come toward me.

I still kept yelling, because I thought the Christians would wake up and realize what was happening to them. Instead, many of them started reaching for their arrows to shoot at me. The others just hesitated, as if they did not know what to make of me. I knew then that I had spoken out prematurely, and that it had been a very foolish mistake.

The Battle Begins

Then I turned and saw the army of the Lord standing behind me. There were thousands of soldiers, but they were still greatly outnumbered. I was shocked and disheartened, for it seemed there were actually many more Christians being used by the evil one than there were in the army of the Lord. I also knew that the battle about to begin was going to be viewed as The Great Christian Civil War, because very few would understand the dark powers that were behind the impending conflict.

As I looked more closely at the army of the Lord, the situation seemed even more discouraging. Only a small number were fully dressed in their armor. Many only had one or two pieces of their armor on; some did not have any at all. A large number were already wounded. Most of those who had all their armor still had very small shields, which I knew would not protect them from the onslaught that was coming. Very few of those who were fully armed were adequately trained to use their weapons. To my further surprise, the great majority of these soldiers were women and children.

Behind this army was a trailing mob, which seemed very different in nature from the prisoners who followed the evil horde. Those in the mob seemed overly happy, as if intoxicated. They were playing games, singing songs, feasting and roaming about from one little camp to the next. This reminded me of Woodstock.

I ran toward the army of the Lord to escape the onslaught I knew would be coming at me from the evil horde. In every way, it seemed we were in for a most one-sided slaughter. I was especially concerned for the mob that was trailing the Lord's army, so I tried to raise my voice above the clamor to warn them that a battle was about to begin. Only a few could even hear me. Those who heard gave me the "peace sign" and said they did not believe in war.

When those in the mob assured me that the Lord would not let anything bad happen to them, I tried to explain that He had given us armor because we needed it for what was about to take place. To this they retorted that they had come to a place of peace and joy where nothing like that could happen to them. I began praying earnestly for the Lord to increase the shields of those with the armor, to help protect those who were not ready for the battle.

Then a messenger came up to me, gave me a trumpet, and told me to blow it quickly. When I did, those who had at least some of their armor on immediately responded, snapping to attention. More armor was brought to them, which they quickly put on.

I noticed that those who were wounded did not put armor over their wounds. But before I could say anything about this, enemy arrows began raining down on us. Everyone who did not have all of his armor on was wounded. Those who had not covered their wounds were struck again in the same area they had been wounded in before.

Those who were hit by arrows of slander immediately began to slander those who were not wounded. Those who were hit with gossip began to gossip, and soon a major division had been created within our own camp. I felt that we were on the verge of destroying ourselves, just as some of the heathen armies in Scripture had done by rising up to kill each other. The feeling of helplessness was terrible.

The Vultures Appear

Then vultures swooped down to pick up the wounded and deliver them into the camp of prisoners. The wounded still had swords and could have easily struck down the vultures, but they didn't. They were actually carried off willingly because they were so angry at those who were not wounded like they were.

I quickly thought about the mob behind the army and ran to see what had happened to them. It seemed impossible, but the scene among them was even worse. Thousands lay on the ground, wounded and groaning. The sky over them was darkened by the vultures that were carrying them off to become prisoners of the enemy.

Many of those who were not wounded just sat in a stupor of unbelief. They, too, were easily carried away by the vultures. Even though a few had begun trying to fight off the vultures, since they did not have the proper weapons, the vultures did not even pay them any attention. The wounded were so angry they would threaten and drive away anyone who tried to help them, but they became docile and submissive to the vultures.

Those who had not been wounded soon gave up trying to fight off the vultures and began running from the scene of battle. This first encounter with the enemy was so devastating that I was tempted to join them in their flight. Then, incredibly fast, some of those who had fled began reappearing with full suits of armor on, holding large shields. This was the first bit of encouragement that I re-member seeing.

These warriors who were returning no longer had the mirth of the party, but an awesome resolve had now replaced it. I knew that although these had been deceived once, they would not be easily deceived again. They began to take the places of those who had fallen, and even began forming new ranks to protect the rear and flanks.

This caused such great courage to spread through the army that the determination of everyone to stand and fight again began to rise. Three great angels named Faith, Hope and Love immediately came and stood behind the army. As we looked at them, all of our shields began to grow. It was amazing how quickly despair had turned to faith. It was a solid faith, too, tempered by experience.

The High Way

Now everyone had swords named "The Word of God" and arrows named for different biblical truths. We wanted to shoot back, but we did not know how to avoid hitting the Christians who were being ridden by the demons. Then it occurred to us that if these Christians were hit with Truth, they would wake up and fight off their oppressors. I fired off a few arrows, as did some of the others. Almost all the arrows hit Christians. However, when the arrow of Truth went into them, they did not wake up or fall down wounded—they became enraged, and the demon riding on them grew much larger.

This shocked everyone, and we began to feel that this was an impossible battle to win. Even so, with Faith, Hope and Love we were confident that we could at least hold our own ground. Another great angel named Wisdom then appeared and directed us to fight from the mountain behind us.

On the mountain were ledges at different levels, for as high as we could see. At each higher level the ledges became narrower and more difficult to stand on. Each level was named for a biblical truth. The lower levels were named after foundational truths such as "Salvation," "Sanctification," "Prayer" and "Faith," and the higher levels were named after deeper biblical truths. The higher we climbed, the larger both our shields and our swords grew, and fewer of the enemy arrows could reach our positions.

Some who had stayed on the lower levels began picking up the enemy arrows and shooting them back. This was a very grave mistake. The demons easily dodged the arrows and let them hit the Christians. When a Christian was hit by one of the arrows of accusation or slander, a demon of bitterness or rage would fly in and perch on that arrow. He would then begin to urinate and defecate his poison upon that Christian. When a Christian had two or three of these demons added to the pride or self-righteousness he already had, he was transformed into the contorted image of the demons themselves.

We could see this happening from the higher levels, but those on the lower levels who were using the enemy's arrows could not see it. About half of us decided to keep climbing, while the other half descended back to the lower levels to explain to those below what was happening. Everyone was then warned to keep climbing and not stop, except for a few who stationed themselves on each level to keep the other soldiers moving higher.

Safety at Last

When we reached the level called "The Unity of the Brethren," none of the enemy's arrows could reach us. Many in our camp decided that this was as far as they needed to climb. I understood this, because with each new level the footing was more precarious. However, I also felt much stronger and more skillful with my weapons as I went higher, so I continued climbing.

Soon my skills were good enough to shoot and hit the demons without hitting the Christians. I felt that if I kept going higher I could shoot far enough to hit the main leaders of the evil horde who stayed behind their army. I regretted that so many had stopped on the lower levels where they were safe but could not hit the enemy. Meanwhile, the strength and character that grew in those who kept climbing made them great champions, each one able to destroy many of the enemy.

At each level there were arrows of Truth scattered about, which I knew were left from those who had fallen from that position. All these arrows were named after the Truth of a certain level, and from each of the levels many people had fallen. Some of those with me were reluctant to pick up these arrows, but I knew we needed all we could get in order to destroy the great horde below.

I picked up one of the arrows, shot it, and so easily hit a demon that the others also started picking up arrows and shooting them. We began to decimate several of the enemy divisions. Because of this, the entire evil army focused its attention on us. For a time it seemed that the more we achieved, the more the enemy attacked us. Though our task seemed endless, it had become exhilarating.

Since the enemy forces could not hit us with their arrows on the higher levels, swarms of vultures would fly above us to vomit down on us. Other vultures carried demons that would urinate or defecate upon the ledges, making them very slippery.

Our swords grew after we reached each new level, but I almost left mine behind because I did not seem to need it at the higher levels. I almost casually decided to keep it, thinking that it must have been given to me for a reason. Then, because the ledge I was standing on was so narrow and slippery, I drove the sword into the ground and tied myself to it while I shot at the enemy.

The voice of the Lord then came to me, saying: *"You have used the wisdom that will enable you to keep climbing. Many have fallen because they did not use their sword properly to anchor themselves."* No one else seemed to hear this voice, but many saw what I had done and did the same.

I wondered why the Lord had not spoken to me to do this sooner. Then I realized that indeed He had already spoken this to me somehow. As I pondered this, I began to understand that my whole life had been training for this hour. I knew that I was prepared to the degree that I had listened to the Lord and obeyed His voice throughout my life. I also knew that for some reason the wisdom and understanding I now had could not be increased or taken away while in this battle. I was very thankful for every trial I had experienced in my life, and I was sorry for not appreciating them more at the time.

27

Soon we were hitting the demons with almost perfect accuracy. Rage ascended from the enemy army like fire and brimstone. I knew that the Christians trapped in that army were now feeling the brunt of that rage. Some of the demons became so enraged that they were now shooting at each other. Normally this would have been very encouraging, but those who suffered the most were the deceived Christians who were in the camp of the enemy. I knew that, to the world, this was appearing as an incomprehensible meltdown of Christianity itself.

Some of those who had not used their swords as anchors were able to strike down many of the vultures, but they were also more easily knocked from the ledges where they were standing. Some of these landed on a lower level, but some fell all the way to the bottom and were picked up and carried off by the vultures. I spent every free moment trying to drive my sword deeper into the ledge, or trying to tie myself more securely to it. Every time I did this, Wisdom would stand beside me, so I knew that it was very important.

A New Weapon

The arrows of Truth would seldom penetrate the vultures, but they hurt them enough to at least drive them back. Every time they were driven back far enough, some of us would climb to the next level. When we reached the level called "Galatians Two Twenty," we were above the altitude that the vultures could withstand. At this level the sky above almost blinded us with its brightness and beauty. I felt peace like I had never felt it before.

Until I reached this level, my fighting spirit had been motivated almost as much by fear, hatred or disgust for the enemy as it had been for the sake of the kingdom, truth or love for the prisoners. But it was on this level I caught up to Faith, Hope and Love, which before I had only been able to see from a distance. Here, I was almost overpowered by their glory. Even so, I felt that I could get close to them.

When I got next to Faith, Hope and Love, they turned to me and began repairing and shining my armor. Soon it was transformed enough to brilliantly reflect the glory that was coming from Faith, Hope and Love. When they touched my sword, great bolts of brilliant lightning began flashing from it.

Love then said, "Those who reach this level are entrusted with the powers of the age to come." Then, turning to me with a seriousness that was very sobering, he said, "I still must teach you how to use them."

The "Galatians Two Twenty" level was so wide that there did not seem to be any danger of falling. An unlimited supply of arrows was available, with the name Hope written on them. We shot some of them down at the vultures, and these arrows killed them easily. About half of those who had reached this level kept shooting, while the others began carrying the arrows down to Christians still on the lower levels.

The vultures kept coming in waves upon the levels below, but with each wave there would be fewer than before. From "Galatians Two Twenty" we could hit any enemy in the army except the leaders themselves, who remained just out of our range. We decided not to use the arrows of truth until we had destroyed all the vultures, because the cloud of depression they created made the truth less effective. This took a very long time, but we did not get tired. Finally, it seemed as if the sky over the mountain was almost completely rid of the vultures.

Just as our weapons had grown, Faith, Hope and Love had also grown with each level. They were now so large that I knew people far beyond the battle area could see them. Their glory even radiated into the camp of prisoners who were still under a great cloud of vultures. I was very encouraged that they could now be seen this way. Maybe now the prisoners and the Christians who had been used by the enemy would understand that *we* were not the enemy, but they in fact had been used by him.

However, this was not to be the case, at least not yet. Those in the camp of the enemy who began to see the light of Faith, Hope and Love started calling them "angels of light" who were sent to deceive the weak or undiscerning. I knew then that their bondage was much greater than I had realized.

The non-Christians, who were not a part of either of these armies, saw the glory of Faith, Hope and Love and started to come closer to the mountain to get a better view. Those who came closer to see them also started to understand what the battle had really been about. This was a great encouragement.

The Trap

The exhilaration of victory continued to grow in each of us. I felt that being in this army and in this battle had to be one of the greatest adventures of all time. After destroying most of the vultures that had been attacking our mountain, we began picking off the vultures that still covered the prisoners. As the cloud of darkness dissipated, the prisoners were bathed in sunlight and began to wake up as if they had been in a deep sleep. They were immediately repulsed by their condition, especially by the vomit that still covered them, and started cleaning themselves up. As they beheld Faith, Hope and Love, they also saw the mountain and ran toward it.

Though the evil horde sent arrows of Accusation and Slander at their backs, the former prisoners did not stop. By the time they got to the mountain many had a dozen or more arrows stuck in them, yet they seemed to not even notice. As soon as they began to scale the mountain, their wounds began to heal. With the cloud of depression largely dispelled, it seemed as if everything was now getting much easier.

The former prisoners had great joy in their salvation. They seemed so overwhelmed with appreciation for each new level of the mountain that it gave us a greater appreciation for those truths too.

Soon a fierce resolve to fight the enemy arose in the former prisoners. They put on the armor provided and begged to be allowed to go back and attack the enemy who had held them captive and abused them for so long. We thought about it, but then decided we should all stay on the mountain to fight.

Again, the voice of the Lord spoke, saying, *"A second time you have chosen wisdom. You cannot win if you try to fight the enemy on his own ground. You must remain on My holy mountain."*

I was stunned that we had made another decision of such importance just by thinking and briefly discussing it. I then resolved to do my best not to make another decision of any consequence without prayer. Wisdom then stepped up to me quickly, took both of my shoulders firmly and looked me straight in the eyes, saying, *"You must do this!"*

As Wisdom said this to me, he pulled me forward as if he were saving me from something. I looked back and saw that, even though I had once been on the broad plateau of "Galatians Two Twenty," I had drifted to the very edge without even knowing it. I had come very close to falling off the mountain. I looked again into the eyes of Wisdom, and he said with the utmost seriousness, *"Take heed when you think you stand, lest you fall. In this life you can fall from any level."*

I thought about Wisdom's words for quite a while. In the exuberance of the victory we were starting to achieve and the unity we were beginning to experience, I had become careless. It was more noble to fall because of the onslaught of the enemy than to fall because of carelessness.

The Serpents

For a long time, we continued killing the vultures and picking off the demons that were riding the Christians. We found that the arrows of different Truths would have greater impact on different demons. We knew that it was going to be a long battle, but we were not suffering any more casualties now, and we had continued to climb past the level of "Patience."

It was troubling that after these Christians had the demons shot off of them, few would come to the mountain. Many had taken on the nature of the demons, and continued in their delusion without them. As the darkness of the demons dissipated, we could see the ground moving around the feet of these Christians. Then I saw that their legs were bound by serpents. As I kept looking at the serpents, I saw that they were all the same kind, and had the name "Shame" written on them.

We shot arrows of Truth at the serpents, but the arrows had little effect. We then tried the arrows of Hope, but without results. From "Galatians Two Twenty" it had been very easy to go higher, because we all helped each other. Since there now seemed to be little that we could do against the enemy, we decided to just try to climb as far as we could until we found something that would work against the serpents.

We passed levels of truth very fast. On most of them we did not even bother to look around if there was no weapon in sight that might work on the serpents. Faith, Hope and Love stayed right with us, but I had not noticed that we had left Wisdom far behind. It would be a long time before I understood what a mistake this was. He would catch up to us on the top, but leaving him behind cost us a much quicker and easier victory over the evil horde.

Almost without warning, we came to a level that opened up into a garden. It was the most beautiful place I had ever seen. Over the entrance to this garden was written, "The Father's Unconditional Love." This entrance was so glorious and inviting that we could not resist entering.

The Beautiful Garden

As soon as I entered the garden, I saw a tree that I knew was the Tree of Life. It was in the middle of this garden, and it was still guarded by angels of awesome power and authority. When I looked at them, they looked back. They seemed friendly, as if they had been expecting us. I looked back, and there was now a host of other warriors in the garden. This gave us all courage, and because of the angels' demeanor we decided to pass them to get to the tree. One of the angels called out, "Those who make it to this level know the Father's love and can eat of the tree."

I did not realize how hungry I was. When I tasted the fruit, it was better than anything I had ever tasted. Yet, it was also familiar somehow. It brought pleasant memories of such things as sunshine, rain, beautiful fields, and the sun setting over the ocean. Even more, it reminded me of the people I loved.

With every bite, I loved everything and everyone more. Then my enemies started coming to mind, and I loved them, too. The feeling was soon greater than anything I had ever experienced, greater even than the peace we felt when we first reached the level of "Galatians Two Twenty."

Then I heard the voice of the Lord, saying, *"This is now your daily bread. It will never be withheld from you. You may eat as much and as often as you like. There is no end to My love."*

I looked up into the tree to see where the voice had come from, and I saw that the tree was filled with pure white eagles. They had the most beautiful, penetrating eyes I have ever seen. They were looking at me as if waiting for instructions.

"They will do your bidding," one of the angels said. "These eagles eat snakes."

"Go!" I told the eagles. "Devour the shame that has bound our brothers."

They opened their wings, and a great wind came and lifted them into the air. The eagles filled the sky with a blinding glory. Even as high as we were, I could hear the sounds of terror from the enemy camp at the sight of the eagles descending.

The Lord Jesus Himself then appeared right in our midst. He took the time to greet each one personally, congratulating us for reaching the top of the mountain. Then He said to us, *"I must now share with you what I shared with your brothers after My resurrection—the message of My kingdom. The enemy's most powerful army has now been put to flight, but not destroyed. Now it is time for us to march forth with the gospel of My kingdom. The eagles have been released and will go with us. We will take arrows from every level, but remember that I am your Sword and your Captain. It is now time for the Sword of the Lord to be unsheathed."*

I then turned and saw that the entire army of the Lord was standing in the garden. There were men, women and children from all races and nations, each carrying their banners, which moved in the wind with perfect unity. I knew that nothing like this had been seen on the earth before. Although the enemy had many more armies and fortresses throughout the earth, I knew that none could stand before this great army of God.

Almost under my breath, I said, "This must be the day of the Lord." To my amazement, the whole host then answered in an awesome thunder, "The day of the Lord of Hosts has come!"

Reflecting on the Dream

Months later, I sat pondering this dream. Alarmingly, certain events and conditions in the church had already seemed to parallel what I had seen when the hordes from hell had begun to march. I was then reminded of Abraham Lincoln. The only way he could become a great emancipator and the preserver of the Union was to be willing to fight a

Civil War. Not only did he have to fight it, but he had to be determined not to compromise until the victory was complete.

Lincoln also had to have the grace to fight the bloodiest war in our history without "demonizing" the enemy with propaganda. If he had done that, he might have been able to galvanize the resolve of the North much faster, facilitating a quicker military victory. However, it would have made the reunion after the war much more difficult. Because he was truly fighting to preserve the Union, Lincoln never made the men and women of the South the enemy, but rather the evil that held them in bondage.

A great spiritual civil war now looms before the church. Many will do everything they can to avoid it. This is understandable, and even noble. However, compromise will never maintain a lasting peace. It will only make the ultimate conflict that much more difficult when it comes—and come it will.

The Lord is now preparing courageous leaders who will be willing to fight a spiritual civil war in order to set men free. The main issue, as in the American Civil War, will be slavery versus freedom. The secondary issue, which will be the primary issue for some, will be money.

Just as the American Civil War at times looked like it would destroy the entire nation, that which is coming upon the church will sometimes appear as if it will bring the end of the church. However, just as the United States not only survived but went on to become the most powerful nation on earth, the same is going to happen to the church. The church will not be destroyed, but the institutions and doctrines that have kept men in spiritual slavery will be.

Even after this, perfect justice in the church will not be attained overnight. There will still be struggles for women's rights and setting the church free from racism and exploitation. These are all causes that must be confronted. Yet, in the midst of the coming spiritual civil war, Faith, Hope and Love—and the kingdom of God they stand upon—will begin to be seen as they never have before. This will begin drawing people to the kingdom. God's government is about to be demonstrated as greater than any human government.

Let us always remember that with the Lord "a thousand years is as a day." He can do in us in one day what we think would take a thousand years. The work of liberating and raising up the church will be accomplished much quicker than we may think is humanly possible. However, we are not talking about human possibilities.

PART II

the holy mountain

We stood in the Garden of God under the Tree of Life. It seemed that the entire army was there, many of them kneeling before the Lord Jesus. He had just given us the charge to return to the battle for the sake of our brothers who were still bound and for the world that He loved. It was both a wonderful and a terrible command. It was wonderful because it came from Him. It was terrible because it meant that we would have to leave His manifest presence and the Garden that was more beautiful than any place we had ever been before. To leave all of this to go into battle again seemed incomprehensible.

The Lord continued His exhortation: *"I have given you spiritual gifts and power, and an increasing understanding of My word and My kingdom, but the greatest weapon you have been given is the*

Father's love. As long as you walk in My Father's love, you will never fail. The fruit of this tree is the Father's love which is manifested in Me. This love, which is in Me, must be your daily bread."

In this setting of such beauty and glory, it did not seem that the Lord was appearing in His glory. In fact, His appearance was rather ordinary. Even so, the grace with which He moved and spoke made Him the most attractive person I had ever seen. He was beyond human definition in dignity and nobility. It was easy to understand why He is everything that the Father loves and esteems. Seeing Him this way, so full of grace and truth, made it seem that nothing but grace and truth should ever matter.

As I ate the fruit from the Tree of Life, the thought of every good thing I had ever known filled my soul. When Jesus spoke, it was the same, only magnified. All I wanted to do was stay in this place and listen to Him. I remembered how I had once thought it must be boring for those angels who do nothing but worship Him continually before the throne. Now I knew that there was nothing more wonderful or exhilarating that we would ever do than to simply worship Him.

Such worship was what we were created for, and it would surely be the best part of heaven. I could not imagine how wonderful it would be if all of the heavenly choirs were added. It was hard to believe that I had struggled so much with boredom during worship services. I knew that it was only because I had been almost completely out of touch with this heavenly reality during those times.

I was almost overwhelmed with the desire to go back and make up those times during worship services when I had allowed my mind to wander or had occupied myself with other things. The desire to express my adoration for Him became almost insatiable. I had to praise Him! As I opened my mouth, I was shocked by the spontaneous worship that erupted from the entire army at the same time. I had almost forgotten that anyone else was there, yet we were all in perfect unity. The glorious worship that followed could not be described in human language.

As we worshiped, a golden glow began to emanate from the Lord. Then silver appeared around the gold. After that, we were all enveloped in colors, the richness of which I have never seen with my natural eyes. With this glory, I entered a realm of emotion that I had never experienced before. Somehow I understood that this glory had been there all along, but when we focused on Him the way we did in worship, we began to see more of His glory. The more intensely we worshiped, the more glory we beheld. If this was heaven, it was much, much better than I had ever dreamed.

His Dwelling Place

I have no idea how long this worship lasted. It could have been minutes, or it could have been months. There was just no way to measure time in that kind of glory. I closed my eyes, because the glory I was seeing with my heart was as great as what I was seeing with my physical eyes.

When I opened my eyes, I was surprised to see that the Lord was not there any longer, but a troop of angels was standing where He had been. One of them approached me and said, "Close your eyes again." When I did, I beheld the glory of the Lord. This was no small relief. Now that I had experienced the glory, I knew that I simply could not live without it.

Then the angel explained, "What you see with the eyes of your heart is more real than what you see with your physical eyes."

I had made this statement myself many times, but how little I had walked in it! The angel continued, "It was for this reason that the Lord told His first disciples it was better for Him to go away so the Holy Spirit could come. The Lord dwells within you. You have taught this many times, but now you must live it; for you have eaten from the Tree of Life."

The angel then began to lead me back to the gate. I protested that I did not want to leave. Seeming surprised, the angel took me by the shoulders and looked me in the eyes. This was when I recognized him—it was Wisdom.

"You never have to leave this garden," he assured me. *"This garden is in your heart because the Creator Himself is within you. You have desired the best part, to worship and sit in His presence forever, and it will never be taken from you. But you must take it from here to where it is needed most."*

I knew he was right. I then looked past him to the Tree of Life. I had a compulsion to grab all of the fruit that I could before leaving. Knowing my thoughts, Wisdom gently shook me. *"No. Even this fruit, gathered in fear, would go bad. This fruit and this tree are within you because He is in you. You must believe."*

Seeing With Eyes Closed

I closed my eyes and tried to see the Lord again, but I couldn't. When I opened my eyes, Wisdom was still staring at me. With great patience, he continued:

"You have tasted of the heavenly realm, and no one ever wants to go back to the battle once they do. No one ever wants to leave the manifest presence of the Lord. After the apostle Paul came here, he struggled for the rest of his life as to whether he should stay and labor for the sake of the church or return here to enter into His inheritance. But his inheritance was magnified the longer he stayed and served on earth. Now that you have the heart of a true worshiper, you will

always want to be here—and you can, whenever you enter into true worship. The more focused you are on Him, the more glory you will see, regardless of where you are."

Wisdom's words had finally calmed me. Again I closed my eyes just to thank the Lord for this wonderful experience, and the life He had given to me. As I did, I started to see His glory again, and all of the emotion of the previous worship experience flooded my soul.

The Lord's words to me were so loud and clear that I was sure they were audible: *"I will never leave or forsake you."*

"Lord, forgive my unbelief," I responded. "Please help me never to leave or forsake *You.*" This was both a wonderful and trying time. Here the "real world" was not real, and the spiritual realm was so much more real that I just could not imagine going back to the other. I was gripped both with wonder and a terrible fear that I might wake up at any moment and find it was all just a dream.

Wisdom understood what was going on inside of me. *"You are dreaming,"* he said. *"But this dream is more real than what you think of as real. The Father gave men dreams to help them see the door to His dwelling place. He will only dwell in men's hearts, and dreams can be a door to your heart, which will lead you to Him. That is why His angels so often appear to men in their dreams. In dreams they can bypass the fallen mind of man and go straight to his heart."*

As I opened my eyes, Wisdom was still gripping my shoulders. *"I am the primary gift that has been given to you for your work,"* he said. *"I will show you the way and keep you on it, but only love will keep you faithful. The fear of the Lord is the beginning of wisdom, but the highest wisdom is to love Him."*

Then Wisdom released me and started to walk toward the gate. I followed with ambivalence. I remembered the exhilaration of the battle and the climb up the mountain, and though it was compelling, there was no comparison to the presence of the Lord and the worship I had just experienced. Leaving this would be the greatest sacrifice I had ever made. Then I remembered how it was all inside of me, and I was amazed that I could forget this so quickly. It was as if a great battle was raging within me, between what I saw with my physical eyes and what I saw with my heart.

The Third Heaven

Having moved forward so that I was walking beside Wisdom, I asked him, "I have prayed for twenty-five years to be caught up into the third heaven like the apostle Paul. Is this the third heaven?"

"This is part of it," he replied, *"but there is much more."*

"Will I be allowed to see more?" I asked.

"You will see much more. I am taking you to see more now," he replied.

I started thinking of the book of Revelation. "Was John's revelation part of the third heaven?" I asked.

"Part of John's revelation was from the third heaven, but most of it was from the second heaven. The first heaven was before the fall of man. The second heaven is the spiritual realm during the reign of evil upon the earth. The third heaven is when the love and domain of the Father will again prevail over the earth through the King."

"What was the first heaven like?" I inquired, strangely feeling a cold chill as I asked.

"It is wisdom not to be concerned about that now," Wisdom responded with increased seriousness, as my question seemed to jolt him. *"Wisdom is to seek to know the third heaven just as you have. There is much more to know about the third heaven than you can know in this life, yet it is the third heaven, the kingdom, that you must preach in this life. In the ages to come you will be told about the first heaven, but it is not profitable for you to know about it now."*

When I resolved to remember the cold chill I had just felt, Wisdom nodded, which I knew to be an affirmation of that thought. "What a great companion you are," I had to say as I realized the valuable gift that this angel was. "You really will keep me on the right path."

"I will indeed," he replied.

The Other Half of Love

I was sure I felt love coming from this angel, which was unique, since I had never felt this from other angels. They usually showed their concern more out of duty than love. Wisdom responded to my thoughts as if I had spoken them out loud.

"It is wisdom to love, and I could not be Wisdom if I did not love you. It is also wisdom to behold the kindness and the severity of God. It is wisdom to love Him and to fear Him. You are in deception if you do otherwise. This is the next lesson that you must learn," he said with unmistakable earnestness.

"I do know that, and have taught it many times," I responded, feeling for the first time that maybe Wisdom did not fully know me.

"I have been your companion for a very long time, and I know your teachings," Wisdom replied. *"Now you are about to learn what some of your own teachings mean. As you have said many times, 'It is not by believing in your mind, but in your heart that results in righteousness.'"*

51

I apologized, feeling a bit ashamed at having questioned Wisdom. He graciously accepted my apology. It was then that I realized I had been questioning and challenging him most of my life, and often to my harm.

"Just as there is a time to plant and a time to reap," Wisdom continued, *"there are times to adore the Lord, and there are times to honor Him with the greatest fear and respect. It is wisdom to know the time for each. True wisdom knows the times and seasons of God. I brought you here because it was time to worship the Lord in the glory of His love. This is what you needed the most after such a battle. I am now taking you to another place because it is time for you to worship Him in the fear of His judgment. Until you know both, there is a danger that we can be separated from each other."*

"Do you mean that if I had stayed back there in that glorious worship I would have lost you?" I asked in disbelief.

"Yes. I would have always visited with you when I could, but we would have rarely crossed paths. Although it is hard to leave such glory and peace, that is not the whole revelation of the King. He is both a Lion and a Lamb. To the spiritual children, He is the Lamb. To the maturing, He is the Lion. To the fully mature, He is both the Lion and the Lamb. Again, I know you understand this, but you have known it primarily in your mind. Soon you will know it in your heart, for you are about to experience the judgment seat of Christ."

Returning to the Battle

Before leaving the gates to the Garden, I asked Wisdom if I could just sit for a while to ponder all that I had just experienced. *"Yes, you should do this,"* he replied, *"but I have a better place for you to do it."*

I followed Wisdom out of the gates, and we began to go down the mountain. To my surprise, the battle was still going on, but not as intensely as it was when we ascended. There were still arrows of accusation and slander flying about on the lower levels, but most of the enemy horde that remained was furiously attacking the great white eagles. The eagles were easily prevailing.

We kept descending until we were almost at the bottom. Just above the levels of "Salvation" and "Sanctification" was the level "Thanksgiving and Praise." I remembered this level very well because one of the greatest attacks of the enemy came when I had first tried to reach it. Once we had gotten here, the rest of the climb was much easier, and when an arrow penetrated our armor, healing came much faster.

As soon as my enemies spotted me on this level (they could not see Wisdom), a shower of arrows began to rain down on me. I knocked them down with my shield so easily that the enemies quit shooting. Their arrows were now almost gone, and they could not afford to waste them.

The soldiers who were still fighting from this level looked at me in astonishment, with a deference that made me very uncomfortable. It was then I first noticed that the glory of the Lord was emanating from my armor and shield. I told these soldiers to climb to the top of the mountain without stopping, and they, too, would see the Lord. As soon as they agreed to go, they saw Wisdom. They started to fall down to worship him, but he restrained them and sent them on their way.

The Faithful

I was filled with love for these soldiers, many of whom were women and children. Their armor was a mess, and they were covered in blood—but they had not given up. In fact, they were still cheerful and encouraged. I told them that they were deserving of more honor than I was, because they had borne the greatest burden of the battle and had held their ground. They seemed not to believe me, but appreciated that I would say it. However, I really felt that it was true.

Every level on the mountain had to be occupied, or the vultures that were left would come and desecrate it with vomit and excrement until it was difficult to stand on. Most of the ledges were occupied by soldiers I recognized to be from different denominations or movements which emphasized the truth of the level they were defending. I was embarrassed by the attitude I had maintained toward some of these groups. I had considered them out of touch and backslidden at best, but here they were fighting faithfully against a terrible onslaught of the enemy. Their defense of these positions had probably enabled me to keep climbing as I had.

Some of these levels were situated so that there was a good view of the mountain and the battlefield, but some were so isolated that the soldiers on them could see only their own position. These seemed unaware of the rest of the battle that was raging, or the rest of the army that was also fighting the battle. They were so wounded from the slander and accusations that they would resist anyone who came down to them from a higher level to encourage them to climb higher.

However, when some came down from the top reflecting the glory of the Lord, the wounded warriors listened, most of them with great joy. Soon a number of them began to climb with courage and resolve. As I beheld all of this, Wisdom did not say much, but he seemed very interested in my reactions.

Reality Discovered

I watched as many soldiers who had been to the top began descending to all of the levels in order to relieve those who had been taking their stand on those truths. As they did, each level began to shine with the glory they carried. Soon the whole mountain was shining with a glory that was blinding to the vultures and demons that were left. After a time, there was so much glory on the mountain that it began to have the same feel as the Garden.

I started thanking and praising the Lord, and immediately I was in His presence again. It was hard to contain the emotions and glory that I felt when I did this. The experience became so intense that I stopped. Wisdom was standing beside me. Putting his hand on my shoulder, he said, *"You enter His gates with thanksgiving, His courts with praise."*

"But that was so real!" I exclaimed. "I felt as if I were there again."

"You were there, indeed," replied Wisdom. *"It has not gotten more real, but you have. Just as the Lord told the thief on the cross, 'Today you will be with Me in Paradise,' you can enter Paradise at anytime. The Lord, His Paradise, and this mountain are all abiding in you, because He is in you. What were but foretastes before are now a reality to you because you have climbed the mountain. The reason you can see me and others can't, is not because I have entered your realm, but because you have entered mine. This is the reality that the prophets knew, which gave them great boldness even when they stood alone against armies. They saw the heavenly host that was for them, not just the earthly one arrayed against them."*

The Deadly Trap

I then looked out over the carnage below and the slowly retreating demonic army. Behind me, more of the glorious warriors were constantly taking their places on the mountain. I knew that we were now strong enough to attack and destroy what was left of this enemy horde. *"Not yet,"* said Wisdom. *"Look over there."*

I looked in the direction in which he was pointing, but had to shield my eyes from the glory emanating from my own armor to see anything. Then I caught a glimpse of some movement in a small valley. I could not make out what I was seeing, because the glory shining from my armor made it difficult to see into the darkness. I asked Wisdom if there was something that I could cover my armor with so I could see it. He then gave me a very plain mantle to put on.

"What is this?" I inquired, a little insulted by its drabness.

"Humility," said Wisdom. *"You will not be able to see very well without it."*

Reluctantly I put it on, and I immediately saw many things that I could not see before. I looked toward the valley and the movement I had seen. To my astonishment, there was an entire division of the enemy horde that was waiting to ambush anyone who ventured from the mountain.

"What army is that?" I asked, "and how did they escape the battle intact?"

"That is Pride," explained Wisdom. *"That is the hardest enemy to see after you have been in the glory. Those who refuse to put on this cloak will suffer much at the hands of that most devious enemy."*

As I looked back at the mountain, I saw many of the glorious warriors crossing the plain to attack the remnant of the enemy horde. None of them were wearing the cloaks of humility, and they had not seen the enemy that was ready to attack them from their rear. I started to run out to stop them, but Wisdom restrained me.

"You cannot stop this," he said. *"Only the soldiers who wear this cloak will recognize your authority. Come with me. There is something else that you must see before you can help lead in the great battle that is to come."*

The Foundation of Glory

Wisdom led me down the mountain to the very lowest level, which was named "Salvation." *"You see this as the lowest level,"* declared Wisdom, *"but this is the foundation of the whole mountain. In any journey, the first step is the most important, and it is usually the most difficult. Without 'Salvation' there would be no mountain."*

I was appalled by the carnage on this level. Every soldier was very badly wounded, but none of them were dead. Multitudes were barely clinging to the edge. Many seemed ready to fall off, but none did. Angels were everywhere ministering to the soldiers with such great joy that I had to ask, "Why are they so happy?"

"These angels have beheld the courage that it took for these to hold on. They may not have gone any further, but neither did they give up. They will soon be healed; then they will behold the glory of the rest of the mountain, and they will begin to climb. These will be great warriors for the battle to come."

"But wouldn't they have been better off to climb the mountain with the rest of us?" I protested, seeing their present condition.

"It would have been better for them, but not for you. By staying here, they kept most of your enemies occupied, and that made it easier for you to climb. Very few from the higher levels ever reached out to help others come to the mountain, but these did. Even when barely clinging to the mountain themselves, they would reach out to pull others up. In fact, most of the mighty warriors were led to the mountain by these faithful ones.

"These who stayed and faithfully fought on the level of Salvation are no less heroes than the ones who made it to the top. They brought great joy to heaven by leading others to salvation. It

was for this reason that all the angels in heaven wanted to come to minister to them, but only the most honored were permitted."

Again I felt shame for my previous attitude toward these great saints. Many of us had scorned them as we climbed to the higher levels. They had made many mistakes during the battle, but they had also displayed more of the Shepherd's heart than the rest of us. The Lord would leave the ninety-nine to go after the one who was lost. These had stayed in the place where they could still reach the lost, and they paid a dear price for it. I, too, wanted to help but did not know where to start.

Wisdom then said, *"It is right for you to want to help, but you will help most by going on to what you have been called to do. These will all be healed and will climb the mountain. They can now climb faster because of you and the others who went before them, both destroying the enemy and marking the way. They will join you again in the battle. These are fearless ones who will never retreat before the enemy."*

The Power of Pride

I was pondering how I was learning as much by descending the mountain as I had by climbing it, when the noise from the battlefield drew my attention. By now there were thousands of the mighty warriors who had crossed the plain to attack the remnant of the enemy horde.

The enemy was fleeing in all directions, except for the one division—Pride. Completely undetected, it had marched right up to the rear of the advancing warriors and was about to release a hail of arrows. I then noticed that the mighty warriors had no armor on their backsides. They were totally exposed and vulnerable to what was about to hit them.

Wisdom remarked, *"You have taught that there was no armor for the backside, which meant that you were vulnerable if you ran from the enemy. However, you never saw how advancing in pride also made you vulnerable."*

I could only nod in acknowledgment, for it was too late to do anything. It was almost unbearable to watch, but Wisdom said that I must. I knew that the kingdom of God was about to suffer a major defeat. Though I had felt sorrow before, I had never felt this kind of sorrow.

To my amazement, when the arrows of pride struck the warriors they did not even notice. However, the enemy kept shooting. The warriors were bleeding and getting weaker fast, but they would not acknowledge it. Soon they were too weak to hold up their shields and swords; they cast them down, declaring that they no longer needed them. Then they started taking off their armor, saying it was not needed anymore either.

Another enemy division appeared and moved up swiftly. It was called Strong Delusion. Its members released a hail of arrows, and they all seemed to hit their mark. It only took a few of the demons of delusion, who were all small and seemingly weak, to lead away this once great army of glorious warriors. They were taken to various prison camps, each named after a different doctrine of demons. I was astounded at how this great company of the righteous had been so easily defeated, and they still did not even know what had hit them.

I blurted out, "How could those who were so strong, who have been all the way to the top of the mountain, who have seen the Lord as they have, be so vulnerable?"

"Pride is the hardest enemy to see, and it always sneaks up behind you," Wisdom lamented. *"In some ways, those who have been to the greatest heights are in the greatest danger of falling. You must always remember that in this life you can fall at any time from any level."*

"Take heed when you think you stand, lest you fall," I replied. "How awesome such Scriptures seem to me now!"

"When you think you are the least vulnerable to falling is in fact when you are the most vulnerable. Most men fall immediately after a great victory," Wisdom lamented.

"How can we keep from being attacked like this?" I asked.

"Stay close to me, inquire of the Lord before making major decisions, and keep that mantle on. Then the enemy will not be able to easily blindside you, as he did them."

I looked at my mantle. It looked so plain and insignificant. I felt that it made me look more like a homeless person than a warrior. Wisdom responded as if I had been speaking out loud.

"The Lord is closer to the homeless than to kings. You only have true strength to the degree that you walk in the grace of God, and 'He gives His grace to the humble.' No evil weapon can penetrate this mantle, because nothing can overpower His grace. As long as you wear this mantle, you are safe from this kind of attack."

I then started to look up to see how many warriors were still on the mountain. I was shocked to see how few there were. I noticed, however, that they all had on the same mantle of humility. "How did that happen?" I inquired.

"When they saw the battle you just witnessed, they all came to me for help, and I gave them their mantles," Wisdom replied.

"But I thought you were with me that whole time?"

"I am with all who go forth to do the will of My Father," Wisdom answered.

"You're the Lord!" I cried.

"Yes," He answered. *"I told you that I would never leave you or forsake you. I am with all My warriors just as I am with you. I will be to you whatever you need to accomplish My will, and you have needed wisdom."* Then He vanished.

Rank in the Kingdom

I was left standing in the midst of the great company of angels who were ministering to the wounded on the level of "Salvation." As I began to walk past these angels, they bowed to one knee and showed me great respect. I finally asked one of them why they did this, as even the smallest was much more powerful than I was. "Because of the mantle," he replied. "That is the highest rank in the kingdom."

"This is just a plain mantle," I protested.

"No!" the angel protested. "You are clothed in the grace of God. There is no greater power than that!"

"But there are thousands of us all wearing the same mantle. How could it represent rank?" I asked.

"You are the dreaded champions, the sons and daughters of the King. He wore the same mantle when He walked on this earth. As long as you are clothed in that, there is no power in heaven or on earth that can stand before you. Everyone in heaven and hell recognizes that mantle. We are indeed His servants, but He abides in you, and you are clothed in His grace."

Somehow I knew that if I had not been wearing the mantle—and my glorious armor had been exposed—the angel's statements and behavior toward me would have fed my pride. It was simply impossible to feel prideful or arrogant while wearing such a drab, plain cloak. However, my confidence in the mantle was growing fast.

PART III

the return of the eagles

On the horizon I saw a great white cloud approaching. Hope rose in me just from seeing it. Soon it had filled the whole atmosphere with hope, just as the rising sun chases away the darkness of night. As it grew closer, I recognized the great white eagles that had flown from the Tree of Life. They began landing on the mountain, taking their places on every level beside the companies of warriors.

I carefully approached the eagle who had landed near me, because his presence was so awesome. When he looked at me with his penetrating eyes, I knew I could hide nothing from him. His eyes were so fierce and resolute that I trembled. Chills ran through me just from looking at them. Before I could even ask, he answered me.

"You want to know who we are. We are the hidden prophets who have been kept for this hour. We are the eyes of those who have been given the divinely powerful weapons. We have been shown all that the Lord is doing, and all that the enemy is planning against you. We have scoured the earth, and together we know all that needs to be known for the battle."

"Did you not see the battle that just took place?" I asked with as much irritation as I dared to express. "Couldn't you have helped those warriors who were just taken captive?"

"Yes," the eagle responded. "We saw it all, and we could have helped if they had wanted our help. We would have helped them by holding them back, telling them to sit and be still. But we can only fight in the battles that the Father commands, and we can only help those who believe in us. Only those who receive us as who we are, the prophets, can receive the prophets' reward, or the benefit of our services. Those who were ambushed did not yet have the mantle that you are wearing, and those who do not have that mantle cannot understand who we are. We all need one another, including these here who are still wounded, and many others who you do not yet know."

The Eagle's Heart

As I talked to the eagle, I started to think like him. After this short discussion I could see into the eagle's heart, and I began to know him like he knew me. The eagle recognized this.

"You have some of our gifts," the eagle noted, "though they are not very well developed. You have not used them much. I am here to awaken these gifts in you, and in many others like you, and I will teach you how to use them. In this way, our communication will be sure. Unless we have sure communication, we will all suffer many unnecessary losses, not to mention missing many great opportunities for victory."

"Where did you just come from?" I asked.

"We eat snakes," the eagle replied. "The enemy is bread for us. Our sustenance comes from doing the Father's will, which is to destroy the works of the devil. Every snake that we eat helps to increase our vision. Every stronghold of the enemy that we tear down strengthens us so we can soar higher and stay in the air longer. We have just come from a feast, devouring the serpents of Shame which have bound many of your brothers and sisters. They will be here soon. They are coming with the eagles we left behind to help them find the way and to protect them from the enemy's counterattacks."

These eagles were very sure of themselves, but not cocky. They knew who they were and what they were called to do. They also knew us and they knew the future. Their confidence was reassuring to me, but even more so to the wounded who were still lying all around us. Those who had recently been too weak to talk were actually sitting up listening to my conversation with the eagle. They looked at him the same way lost children would look to their parents who had just found them.

The Wind of the Spirit

When the eagle looked upon the wounded, his countenance changed as well. In place of the fierce resoluteness he had previously exhibited, he was like a soft, compassionate old grandfather when gazing upon the wounded. The eagle opened his wings and began to gently flap them, stirring up a cool, refreshing breeze that flowed over the wounded. It was unlike any other breeze I had ever felt before. With each breath I was gaining strength and clarity of mind. Soon the wounded were standing and worshiping God with a sincerity that brought tears to my eyes.

Again I felt a profound shame at having scorned those who stayed on this level. They had seemed so weak and foolish to those of us who were ascending the mountain; but they had endured much more than we had, and they remained faithful. God had kept them, and they loved Him with a great love.

I looked up at the mountain. The eagles were all gently flapping their wings. Everyone on the mountain was being refreshed by the breeze they were stirring up, and we all began to worship the Lord. At first there was some discord between the worship coming from the different levels, but soon everyone on every level was singing in perfect harmony.

Never on earth had I heard anything that beautiful. I never wanted it to end. Soon I recognized it as the same worship that we had known in the Garden, but now it sounded even richer and fuller. I knew that it was because we were worshiping in the very presence of our enemies, in the midst of such darkness and evil surrounding the mountain, that it seemed so much more beautiful.

I do not know how long this worship lasted, but eventually the eagles stopped flapping their wings and it stopped. "Why did you stop?" I asked the eagle I had been talking with.

"Because now they are whole," he replied, indicating the wounded, who now were all standing and appeared to be in perfect condition. "True worship can heal any wound," he added.

"Please do it again," I begged.

"We will do this many times, but it is not for us to decide when. The breeze that you felt was the Holy Spirit. He directs us; we do not direct Him. He has healed the wounded and has begun to bring about the unity that is required for the battles ahead. True worship also pours the precious oil upon the Head, Jesus. The oil then flows down over the entire body, making us one with Him and with each other.

"No one who comes into union with Him will remain wounded or unclean. His blood is pure life, and it flows through us when we are joined to Him. And when we are joined to Him we are also joined to the rest of the body, so that His blood flows through us all. Isn't that how you heal a wound to your body, by closing the wound so blood can flow to the wounded member and bring regeneration? When a part of His body is wounded, we must join in unity with that part until it is fully restored. We are all one."

In the euphoria still left from the worship, this brief teaching seemed almost esoteric. Yet I knew it was very basic. When the Holy Spirit moved, every word seemed glorious, regardless of how elementary it was. I was so filled with love that I wanted to hug everyone, including the fierce old eagles.

Then, like a jolt, I remembered the mighty warriors who had just been captured. The eagle sensed this but did not say anything. He just watched me intently. Finally, I spoke up, "Can we recover those who were just lost?"

"Yes. It is right for you to feel what you do," the eagle finally said. "We are not complete, and our worship is not complete, until the whole body is restored. Even in the most glorious worship, in the very presence of the King, we will feel this emptiness until all are one—because our King also feels it.

"We all grieve for our brothers in bondage, but we grieve even more for the heart of our King. Though you love each of your children, you would be particularly concerned for the one who was sick or wounded. The King loves all of His children too, but the wounded and oppressed have most of His attention now. For His sake, we must not quit until all have been recovered. As long as any are wounded, He is wounded."

Faith to Move the Mountain

Sitting down by the eagle, I pondered his words. Finally I remarked, "I know that Wisdom now speaks to me through you, because I hear His voice when you speak. I was so sure of myself before that last battle, but I was almost carried away with the same presumption that they were carried away with.

75

I could very easily have been captured with them if Wisdom had not stopped me.

"I was motivated more by hatred for the enemy than by the desire to set my brothers free. Since coming to this mountain and fighting in the great battle, I now think that most of the right things I did, I did for the wrong reasons; and many of the wrong things I did, I had good motives for. The more I learn, the more unsure of myself I feel."

"You must have been with Wisdom a long time," the eagle responded.

"He was with me a long time before I began to recognize Him, but I am afraid that most of that time I was resisting Him. Somehow I now know I am still lacking something very important, something I must have before I go into battle again—but I do not know what it is."

The great eagle's eyes became even more penetrating as he responded, "You also know the voice of Wisdom when He speaks to you in your own heart. You are learning well, because you have the mantle. What you are feeling now is true faith."

"Faith?" I shot back. "I'm talking about serious doubts!"

"You are wise to doubt yourself. True faith depends on God, not on you and not even on your faith. You are close to the kind of faith that can move this mountain, and move it we must. It is time to carry it to places where it has not traveled before.

"However, you are right that you are still lacking something very important. You must yet have a revelation. Even though you have climbed to the top of the mountain and received from every truth along the way; and have stood in the Garden of God and tasted of His unconditional love; and have seen His Son many times now—you still understand only a part of the whole counsel of God, and that only superficially."

I knew that this was true, and it was actually comforting to hear it. "I have judged so many people and so many situations wrongly!" I exclaimed. "Wisdom has saved my life many times now, but the voice of Wisdom is still a very small voice within me, and the clamor of my own thoughts and feelings are still far too loud. I hear Wisdom speaking through you much louder than I hear Him in my own heart, so I know I must stay very close to you."

"We are here because you need us," the eagle replied. "We are also here because we need you. You have been given gifts I do not have, and I have been given gifts you do not have. You have experienced things I have not experienced, and I have experienced things that you have not. The eagles have been given to you until the end, and you have been given to us. I will be very close to you for a time, and then you must receive other eagles in my place. Every eagle is different. It is together, not individually, that we have been given to know the secrets of the Lord."

The Doors of Truth

The eagle then rose up from the rock on which he had perched and soared over to the edge of the level on which we stood. "Come," he said. As I approached him, I saw steps that led down to the very base of the mountain, and a small door.

"Why have I not seen this before?" I asked.

"When you first came to the mountain you did not stay on this level long enough to look around," he answered.

"How did you know that? Were you here when I first came to the mountain?"

"I would have known if I had not been here, because all who miss this door do so for the same reason," he responded. "But, in fact, I was here. I was one of the soldiers you so quickly passed on your way up the mountain."

It was then that I recognized the eagle as a man I had met and had a few conversations with soon after my conversion. He continued, "I wanted badly to follow you then. I had been on this level for so long that I needed a change. But I just could not leave all the lost souls that I was still trying to lead here. When I finally committed myself to doing the Lord's will, whether it was to stay or go, Wisdom appeared to me and showed me this door. He said it was a shortcut to the top. That is how I got to the top before you did. There I was changed into an eagle."

I then remembered that I had seen doors like this on a couple of the levels. I had even peeked into one of them, and was amazed at what I saw. I did not venture very far into it because I was so focused on the battle and on trying to get to the top of the mountain. "Could I have entered one of those doors and gone right to the top?" I asked.

"It is not quite that easy," the eagle remarked, seeming a little irritated. "In every door there are passageways, one of which leads to the top." Anticipating my next question, he continued, "The other ones lead to the other levels on the mountain. The Father designed each passageway so that everyone would choose the one his level of maturity dictated."

"Incredible! How did He do that?" I thought to myself, but the eagle heard my thoughts.

"It was very simple," continued the eagle, as if I had spoken my thoughts out loud. "Spiritual maturity is always determined by our willingness to sacrifice our own desires for the interests of the kingdom or for the sake of others. The door that requires the most sacrifice to enter will always take us to the highest level."

I was trying to remember all that the eagle was saying to me. I knew I must enter the door before me, and that it would be wise to learn all I could from someone who had preceded me and had obviously chosen the correct door to the top.

"I did not go directly to the top, and I haven't met anyone who has," the eagle continued. "But I went there much faster than most, because I had learned so much about self-sacrifice while fighting here on the level of Salvation. I have shown you this door because you wear the mantle and would have found it anyway. Time is short, and I am here to help you mature quickly."

"There are doors on every level, and every one leads to treasures that are beyond your comprehension," he continued. "They cannot be acquired physically, but every treasure that you hold in your hands you will be able to carry in your heart. Your heart is meant to be the treasure house of God. By the time you reach the top again, your heart will contain treasures more valuable than all the treasures of the earth. They will never be taken from you, but they are yours for eternity. Go quickly. The storm clouds are now gathering, and another great battle is looming."

"Will you go with me?" I pleaded.

"No," he responded. "This is where I belong now. I must help these who were wounded. But I will see you here again. You will meet many of my brother and sister eagles before you return, and they will be able to help you better than I at the place where you meet them."

The Treasures of Heaven

I already loved the eagle so much that I could hardly stand to leave him. I was glad to know I would see him again. Now the door was drawing me like a magnet. I opened it and entered.

The glory that I beheld was so stunning that I immediately fell to my knees. The gold, silver and precious stones were far more beautiful than can be described. They actually rivaled the glory of the Tree of Life. The room was so large that it seemed to be without end. The floor was silver, the pillars were gold, and the ceiling was a single pure diamond that reflected every color I had ever known and many that I had not known. Angels without number were all around, dressed in various robes and uniforms that were of no earthly origin.

As I began to walk through the room, the angels all bowed in salute. One stepped forward and welcomed me by name. He explained that I could go anywhere in the room and see anything I wanted. Nothing was withheld from those who came through the door.

I was so overwhelmed by the beauty that I could not even speak. I finally remarked that this was even more beautiful than the Garden had been. Surprised, the angel responded, "This *is* the Garden! This is one of the rooms in your Father's house. We are your servants."

As I walked, a great company of angels followed me. I turned and asked the leader why they were following. "Because of the mantle," he said. "We have been given to you, to serve you here and in the battle to come."

I did not know what to do with the angels, so I just continued walking. I was attracted to a large blue stone that appeared to have the sun and clouds inside of it. When I touched it, the same feelings flooded over me as when I had eaten the fruit of the Tree of Life. I felt energy, unearthly mental clarity, and love for everyone and everything. I started to behold the glory of the Lord. The longer I touched the stone, the more the glory increased. I never wanted to take my hand off the stone, but the glory became so intense that I finally had to draw away.

Then my eyes fell on a beautiful green stone. "What does that one have in it?" I asked the angel standing nearby.

"All of these stones are the treasures of salvation. You are now touching the heavenly realm, and that one is the restoration of life," he continued.

As I touched the green stone, I began to see the earth in rich and spectacular colors. They grew in richness the longer I had my hand on the stone, and my love for all that I saw also grew. I began to see a harmony among all living things, on a level that I had never seen before. Then I began to see the glory of the Lord in the creation. It began to grow until again I had to step away because of the intensity.

Losing Track of Time

It occurred to me that I had no idea how long I had been there. I did know that my comprehension of God and His universe had grown substantially as I merely touched these two stones—and there were many, many more to touch. There was more in that one room than a person could have absorbed in a whole lifetime. "How many more rooms are there?" I asked the angel.

"There are rooms like this on every level of the mountain you climbed."

"How can one ever experience all that is in just one of these rooms, much less all of them?" I asked.

"You have forever to do this. The treasures contained in the most basic truths of the Lord Jesus are enough to last for more lifetimes than you can measure. No man can know all there is to know about any of them in just one lifetime, but you must take what you need and keep proceeding toward your destiny."

I started thinking about the impending battle again, and the warriors who had been captured. It was not a pleasant thought in such a glorious place, but I knew I would have forever to come back to this room. I had only a short time to find my way back to the top of the mountain and then back to the battlefront again.

I turned back to the angel and said, "You must help me find the door that leads to the top."

The angel looked perplexed. "We are your servants," he responded, "but you must lead us. This whole mountain is a mystery to us. We all desired to look into this great mystery, but after we leave this room we will be learning even more than you."

"Do you know where all the doors are?" I asked.

"Yes. But we do not know where they lead. There are some that look very inviting, some that are plain, and some that are actually repulsive. One is even terrible."

"In this glorious place there are doors that are repulsive?" I asked in disbelief. "And one that is terrible? How can that be?"

"We do not know, but I can show it to you," he responded.

"Please do," I said.

We walked for quite a while, passing treasures of unspeakable glory, all of which were difficult to bypass. There were also many doors, with different biblical truths over each one. When the angel had called them "inviting," I felt that he had quite understated their appeal. I badly wanted to go through each one, but my curiosity about the "terrible door" kept me moving.

Then I saw it. "Terrible" had also been an understatement. Fear gripped me until I thought it would take my breath away.

Gethsemane

I turned away from that door and quickly retreated. There was a beautiful red stone nearby, which I almost lunged at to lay my hands on. Immediately I was in the

Garden of Gethsemane beholding the Lord in prayer. The agony I beheld was even more terrible than the door I had just seen. Shocked, I jerked my hand away from the stone and fell to the floor in exhaustion.

I wanted so badly to return to the blue or green stones, but I had to regain my energy and my sense of direction. The angels were quickly all around me, serving me. I was given a drink that began to revive me. Soon I was feeling well enough to stand and begin walking back to the other stones. However, the recurring vision of the Lord praying finally compelled me to stop.

"What was that back there?" I asked.

"When you touch the stones we are able to see a little of what you see, and feel a little of what you feel," said the angel. "We know that all these stones are great treasures, and the revelations they contain are priceless. We beheld for a moment the agony of the Lord before His crucifixion, and we briefly felt what He felt that terrible night. It is hard for us to understand how our God could ever suffer like that. It makes us appreciate much more what an honor it is to serve the men for whom He paid such a terrible price."

The angel's words were like lightning bolts straight to my soul. I had fought in the great battle. I had climbed to the top of the mountain. I had become so familiar with the spiritual realm that I hardly noticed angels anymore, and I could speak on nearly equal terms with the great eagles. Yet I could not bear to share even a moment of the sufferings of the Lord without wanting to flee to a more pleasurable experience. "I should not be here," I almost shouted. "I, more than anyone, deserve to be a prisoner of the evil one!"

"Sir," the angel said apprehensively, "we understand that no one is here because he deserves it. You are here because you were chosen before the foundation of the world for a purpose. We do not know what your specific purpose is, but we know that it is very great for everyone on this mountain."

"Thank you," I replied. "You are helpful. My emotions are being greatly stretched by this place, and they tend to overcome my understanding. You are right. No one is here because he is worthy. Truly, the higher we climb on this mountain, the more unworthy we are to be here and the more grace we need to stay. How did I ever make it to the top the first time?"

"Grace," my angel responded.

"If you want to help me," I said, "please keep repeating that word to me whenever you see me in confusion or despair. I am coming to understand that word better than any other."

"Now I must go back to the red stone," I continued. "I know now that is the greatest treasure in this room, and I must not leave until I am carrying that treasure in my heart."

The Truth of Grace

The time I spent at the red stone was the most painful ordeal I have ever experienced. Many times I simply could not take anymore but had to withdraw my hand. Several times I went back to the blue or green stones to rejuvenate my soul before I returned. It was harder to return to the red stone each time, but my love for the Lord was growing more through this than anything I had ever learned or experienced.

Finally, when I saw the presence of the Father depart from Jesus on the cross, I could stand it no longer. I quit. I could tell that the angels, who were also experiencing what I was to a degree, were in full agreement with me. The willpower to touch the stone again simply was no longer in me. I did not even feel like going back to the blue stone. I just lay prostrate on the floor, weeping over what the Lord had gone through. I also wept because I knew that I had deserted Him just like His disciples. I failed Him when He needed me the most, just as they did.

After what seemed like several days, I opened my eyes. Another eagle was standing beside me. In front of him were three stones: one blue, one green, and one red.

"Eat them," the eagle said. When I did, my whole being was renewed, and great joy and great soberness both flooded my soul.

When I stood up, I caught sight of the same three stones set into the handle of my sword and on each of my shoulders.

"These are now yours forever," the eagle said. "They cannot be taken from you, and you cannot lose them."

"But I did not finish this last one," I protested.

"Christ alone will ever finish that test," he replied. "You have done well enough, and you must go on now."

"Where to?" I asked.

"You must decide, but with the time getting shorter I will suggest that you try to get to the top soon." The eagle then departed, obviously in a hurry.

I then remembered the doors. I started toward those that had been so appealing. But when I reached the first one, it simply did not appeal to me anymore. Then I went to another, and it felt the same. "Something seems to have changed," I remarked out loud.

"*You* have changed," the angels replied at once.

I turned to look at them and was amazed at how much they had changed. They no longer had a naive look about them, but were now more regal and wise-looking. I knew they reflected what had also taken place in me, but I now felt uncomfortable just thinking about myself.

"I ask for your counsel," I said to the leader.

"Listen to your heart," he said. "That is where these great truths now abide."

"I have never been able to trust my own heart," I responded. "It is subject to so many conflicts. I am too subject to delusions, deceptions and selfish ambitions. It is hard for me to even hear the Lord speaking to me above its clamor."

"Sir, with the red stone now in your heart, I do not believe that will continue to be the case," the leader offered with uncharacteristic confidence.

Judgment's Door

I leaned against the wall, thinking that the eagle was not here when I needed him the most. He had gone this way before and would know which door to choose. But I knew he would not come back, and I knew it was right that I choose. As I pondered my options, the "terrible door" was the only one I could think of. Out of curiosity I decided to go back and look at it. I had departed from it so fast the first time that I had not even noticed which truth it represented.

As I approached it, I could feel the fear welling up inside me, but not nearly as intensely as the first time. Unlike the other doors, it was very dark around this one, and I had to get very close to read the truth written over it. Mildly surprised, I read "THE JUDGMENT SEAT OF CHRIST."

"Why is this truth so fearful?" I asked aloud, knowing that the angels would not answer me. As I continued looking at it, I knew that it was the one I should go through.

"There are many reasons it is fearful," the familiar voice of the eagle responded.

"I'm very glad you came back," I replied. "Have I made a poor choice?"

"No! You have chosen well," the eagle assured me. "This door will take you back to the top of the mountain faster than any other. It is fearful because the greatest fear in the creation has its source through that door. The greatest wisdom that men can know in this life, or in the life to come, is also found through that door. Even so, very few will go through it."

"But why is this door so dark?" I asked.

91

"The light of these doors reflects the attention that the church is presently giving to the truths behind them. The truth behind that door is one of the most neglected of these times, yet it is one of the most important. You will understand when you enter. The greatest authority that men can receive will be entrusted only to those who will go through this door. When you see Christ Jesus sitting on this throne, you will be prepared to sit with Him on it, too."

"Then this door would not be so dark and foreboding if we had just given more attention to this truth?" I asked.

"That is correct. If men knew the glory that is revealed behind that door, it would be one of the most brilliant," the eagle lamented. "However, it is still a difficult door to pass through. I was told to return and encourage you, because soon you will need it. You will see a greater glory, but also a greater terror than you have ever known.

"Because you have chosen the difficult way now, it will be much easier for you later. Because you are willing to face this hard truth now, you will not suffer loss later. Many love to know His kindness, but very few are willing to know His severity. If you do not embrace *both*, you will always be in danger of deception and of a fall from His great grace."

"I know that I would never come here if I had not spent the time I did at the red stone. How could I keep trying to take the easy way, when that is so contrary to the nature of the Lord?" I asked.

"But now you have chosen, so go quickly," the eagle told me. "Another great battle is about to begin, and you are needed at the front," he said.

As I looked at the eagle and saw the great resoluteness in his eyes, my confidence grew. Finally, I turned toward the door.

PART IV

the white throne

I gazed one last time around the huge room inside the mountain. The gems and treasures that represented the truths of Salvation were breathtaking in their glory. It seemed that there was no end to their expanse, and no way to fully comprehend their beauty.

I could not imagine that the rooms which contained the other great truths of the faith could be any more glorious. This helped me to understand why so many Christians never wanted to leave this level, being content to just marvel at the basic doctrines of the faith. I knew that I could stay here for eternity and never get bored.

Then the eagle who was standing next to me exhorted, "You must go on!" As I turned to look at him, he lowered his voice and continued, "There is no greater peace and safety than to abide in the Lord's salvation. You were brought here to know this because you will need this faith for where you are now going. But you must not stay here any longer."

The eagle's statement about peace and safety caused me to think about the courageous warriors who had fought in the battle from the first level of the mountain, Salvation. Although they had fought so well and delivered so many, they had also all been badly wounded. It did not seem that they had found peace and safety here.

The eagle interrupted my thoughts again as if he were listening to them. "God has a different definition of peace and safety than we do," he said. "To be wounded in the fight is a great honor. It is by the Lord's stripes that we are healed, and it is through our stripes that we, too, are given the authority for healing. Once we are healed, we are given the power to heal others in the very place where the enemy wounded us.

"Healing was a basic part of the Lord's ministry, and it is also a basic part of ours. One reason why the Lord allows bad things to happen to His people is so they can receive compassion for others, by which the power of healing operates. That is why the apostle Paul told of his beatings and stonings when his authority was questioned. Every wound and other bad thing that happens to us can be turned into the authority to do good. Every beating that the great apostle took resulted in salvation for others. Every wound that a warrior receives will result in others being saved, healed or restored."

The eagle's words were very encouraging. Standing here amid the glory of the treasures of salvation made this truth even clearer and more penetrating. I wanted to go shout it from the top of the mountain so that all who were still fighting would be encouraged.

Then the eagle continued, "There is another reason why the Lord allows us to be wounded. There is no courage unless there is real danger. The Lord said He would go with Joshua to fight for the Promised Land, but over and over He exhorted him to be strong and courageous. This was because he was going to have to fight, and there would be very real danger. It is in this way that the Lord proves those who are worthy of the Promises."

The Glorious Eagle

I looked at the old eagle, and for the first time I noticed the scars amid his torn and broken feathers. However, the scars were not ugly. They were lined with gold that was somehow not metal, but rather flesh and feathers. I could see that this gold was giving off the glory that emanated from the eagle and made his presence so awesome.

"Why did I not see this before?" I inquired.

"Until you have beheld and appreciated the depths of the treasures of salvation, you cannot see the glory that comes from suffering for the sake of the gospel. Once you have seen it, you are ready for the tests that will release the highest levels of spiritual authority into your life. These scars are the glory that we will carry forever. This is why even the wounds our Lord suffered are with Him in heaven. You can still see His wounds, and the wounds that all of His chosen ones have taken for His sake.

"These are the medals of honor in heaven. All who carry them love God and His truth more than their own lives. These are the ones who followed the Lamb wherever He went, willing to suffer for the sake of truth, righteousness and the salvation of men. True leaders of His people, who carry genuine spiritual authority, must have first proven their devotion this way."

I looked at the leader of the company of angels that followed me. I had never witnessed deep emotion in an angel before, but these words were unquestionably moving him greatly, as well as the rest of the angels. I really thought they were about to cry.

Then the leader spoke: "We have witnessed many wonders since the creation. But the voluntary suffering of men for the Lord and for their fellow men is the greatest wonder of all. We, too, must fight and even suffer at times, but we dwell where there is such light and glory that it is very easy to do this.

"When we see men and women choose to suffer for a hope they can see only dimly in their hearts, it causes even the greatest angels to bow their knee and gladly serve these heirs of salvation. We marvel at the dedication of you who dwell, with so little encouragement, in a place of such darkness and evil.

"At first we did not understand why the Father decreed that men would have to walk by faith, suffering great opposition while not having the benefit of beholding the reality and the glories of the heavenly realm. But now we understand that through these sufferings He proves their worthiness to receive the great authority that they will be given as members of His own household.

"This walk of faith is now the greatest wonder in heaven. Those who pass this test are worthy to sit with the Lamb on His throne, for He has made them worthy and they have proven their love."

Courage

Then the eagle interjected, "Courage is a demonstration of faith. The Lord never promised that His way would be easy, but He has assured us that it would be worth it. The courage of those who fought from the level of Salvation moved the angels of heaven to esteem what God has brought about in fallen men. The faithful warriors took their wounds in the terrible onslaught, while only beholding darkness and a seeming defeat of the truth, just as our Lord did on His cross. Nevertheless, they did not quit, and they did not retreat."

I was again starting to regret that I had not remained on the level of Salvation and fought with those other brave souls. Again, understanding my thoughts, the eagle interrupted them.

"By climbing the mountain, you were demonstrating faith and wisdom, too. Your faith freed many souls so they could come to the mountain for salvation. You received some wounds, as the warriors on the level of Salvation did, but your authority in the kingdom has come more from acts of faith than from suffering. Because you have been faithful in a few things, you will now be given the great honor of going back to suffer, that you may be made a ruler over many more.

"But remember that we all work together for the same purposes regardless of whether we are building or suffering. If you go higher, many more souls will fill these rooms, to the great joy of heaven. You have now been called to climb and to build, but if you are faithful in this you will later be given the honor of suffering."

I then turned and looked at the dark and foreboding door over which was written, *"The Judgment Seat of Christ."* Just as warmth and peace had flooded my soul each time I looked at the great treasures of salvation, fear and insecurity gripped me when I looked at this door. Now it seemed that everything in me wanted to stay in this room, and nothing in me wanted to go through that door.

Again, the eagle answered my thoughts:

"Before you enter the door to any great truth, you will have these same feelings. You even felt them when you entered into this room filled with the treasures of salvation. These fears are the result of the fall. They are the fruit of the Tree of the Knowledge of Good and Evil. The knowledge from that tree made us all insecure and self-centered. The knowledge of good and evil makes the true knowledge of God seem fearsome, when in fact every truth from God leads to an even greater peace and security. Even the judgments of God are to be desired, because all of His ways are perfect."

By now I had experienced enough to know that what seems right is usually the least fruitful path, and is often the road to failure. Throughout my journey, the path of greatest risk was the path that led to the greatest reward. Even so, each time it seemed that more was at stake. Therefore, making the choice to go higher became more difficult each time. I started to sympathize with those who would stop at some point in their sojourn and refuse to go on, even though I knew more than ever that this was a mistake. The only true security came from continually moving forward into the realms that required more faith, which meant more dependence on the Lord.

"Yes, it takes more faith to walk in the higher realms of the Spirit," the eagle added. "The Lord gave us the map to His kingdom when He said, 'If you seek to save your life you will lose it, but if you will lose your life for My sake you will find it.' These words alone can keep you on the path to the top of the mountain and lead you to victory in the great battle ahead. They will also help you stand before the judgment seat of Christ."

Through the Door

I knew it was time for me to go. I resolved to always remember the glory of this chamber that contained the treasures of salvation, but I also knew that I had to move beyond them. I had to go on. I turned, and with all of the courage I could muster, opened the door to the judgment seat of Christ and stepped through it into terrifying darkness. The company of angels that had been assigned to me took positions all around the door, but did not enter.

"What's the matter? Aren't you coming?" I demanded.

"Where you are going now, you must go alone. We will be waiting for you on the other side."

Without responding, I turned and started walking before I could change my mind. Somehow I knew that I should not put my security in the company of angels. As I walked into the darkness, I heard the eagle's parting words,

"After this you will not have your trust in anyone else—even yourself—but only in the Lord."

I immediately was in the most frightening darkness I had ever experienced. Each step became a terrible battle with fear. Soon I began to think I had stepped into hell itself. Finally I decided to retreat, but when I turned to go back, I could not see anything. The door was closed, and I could not even see where it was located. It was beginning to look as if everything that had happened to me, and everything the eagles and the angels had told me, had been a ruse to entrap me in this hell. I had been deceived!

I cried to the Lord to forgive me and help me. Immediately I began to see Him on the cross, just as when I had laid my hand on the red stone in the chamber I had just left. Again I beheld the darkness of His soul as He stood alone, bearing the sin of the world. Although in the chamber this had been a terrible darkness to behold, now it was a light. I resolved that I had to go on, fixing my mind on Him. As I did, peace began to grow in my heart with each step, and it became easier than it had been just a few minutes earlier.

Soon I was not even aware of the chilly darkness, and I started to see a dim light. Gradually it became a glorious light. Then it became so wonderful that I felt I was entering into heaven itself. The glory kept increasing as I walked along, and I wondered how anything this magnificent could have an entrance so dark and foreboding. Now I was enjoying every step.

The Great Hall

The path soon opened into a hall so large that I did not think the earth itself could contain it. Its beauty could not even be described by any reference to human architecture. This exceeded the wonder of anything I had yet experienced, including the garden and the chamber that held the treasures of salvation.

By now I was as overwhelmed with joy and beauty as I had been overwhelmed by darkness and fear just minutes before. I then understood that every time I had experienced great pain or darkness of soul, it had been followed by a much greater revelation of glory and peace.

At the far end was the Source of the glory that was emanating from everything else in the room. I knew that it was the Lord Himself, and though I had now seen Him many times, I began to be a bit afraid as I walked toward Him. However, this fear was a holy fear that only magnified the great joy and peace that I also felt. Not only was the judgment seat of Christ a source of more security than I had ever experienced, but at the same time it was the source of a greater and purer fear.

I did not notice how great the distance was to the throne. It was so wonderful just to walk here that I did not care if it took me a thousand years to get there. In earthly terms, it did take me a very long time. In one sense I felt that it was days, and in another, years. But somehow earthly time had no relevance here.

My eyes were so fixed on the glory of the Lord that I walked a long time before I noticed that I was passing multitudes of people who were standing in ranks to my left (there were just as many to my right, but they were so far away that I could not see them until I reached the throne). As I looked at them, I had to stop. They were dazzling, more regal than anyone I had ever seen. Their countenances were captivating.

Never had such peace and confidence graced human faces. Each one was beautiful beyond any earthly comparison. As I turned toward those who were close to me, they bowed in a greeting as though they recognized me.

"How is it that you know me?" I asked, surprised at my own boldness to ask them a question.

"You are one of the saints fighting in the last battle," a man close by responded. "Everyone here knows you, as well as all those who are now fighting on the earth. We are the saints who have served the Lord in the generations before you. We are the great cloud of witnesses who have been given the right to behold the last battle. We know all of you, and we see all that you do."

To my surprise, I recognized someone I had known on earth. He had been a faithful believer, but I did not think he had ever done anything of significance. He was so unattractive physically on earth that it made him shy. Here he had the same features, but was somehow more handsome than any person I had known on earth. He stepped up to me with an assurance and dignity that I had never seen before in him, or in any man.

"Heaven is much greater than we could have dreamed while on earth," he began. "This room is but the threshold of realms of glory that are far beyond our ability to compre-hend. It is also true that the second death is much more terrible than we understood. Neither heaven nor hell are like we thought they were. If I had known on earth what I know here, I would not have lived the way I did. You are greatly blessed to have been able to come here before you die," he said, looking at my garments.

I then looked at myself. I still had the old mantle of humility on, and the armor was still under it. I felt both foul and crude standing before those who were so glorious. I began to think that I was in serious trouble if I was going to appear before the Lord like this. Like the eagles, my old acquaintance could understand my thoughts, and he responded to them.

"Those who come here wearing that mantle have nothing to fear. That mantle is the highest rank of honor, and it is why they all bowed to you when you passed."

"I did not notice anyone bowing to me," I replied, a bit disconcerted. "In fact, I didn't even notice anyone until just now."

"It is not improper for someone to bow down before you," he continued. "Here we show each other the respect that is due. Even the angels serve us here, but only our God and His Christ are worshiped. There is a marked difference between honoring one another in love, and worshiping them. If we had understood this on earth, we would have treated others very differently. It is here in the light of His glory that we can fully perceive and understand each other, so we can relate properly."

Foolish Virgins

I was still ashamed. I had to restrain myself to keep from bowing down to those in the great hall, while at the same time wanting to hide myself because I felt so lowly. Then I began lamenting the fact that my thoughts here were just as foolish as they were on the earth—and here everyone knew them! I felt both stained and stupid standing before these who were so awesome and pure. Again my old acquaintance responded to these thoughts.

"We have our incorruptible bodies now, and you do not. Our minds are no longer hindered by sin. We are therefore able to easily comprehend what even the greatest earthly mind cannot fathom, and we will spend eternity growing in our ability to understand. This is so we can know the Father and understand the glory of His creation. On earth you cannot even begin to understand what the least of those here knows. In fact, we are the least of those here."

"How could you be the least?" I asked with disbelief.

"There is an aristocracy of sorts here," he answered. "The rewards for our earthly lives are the eternal positions that we will have forever. This great multitude are those whom the Lord called 'foolish virgins.' We knew the Lord and trusted in His cross for salvation, but we lived for ourselves more than we really lived for Him. We did not keep our vessels filled with the oil of the Holy Spirit. We have eternal life, but we wasted our lives on earth."

I was greatly surprised by what he was telling me, but I also knew that no one could lie in that place.

"The foolish virgins gnashed their teeth in the *outer darkness*," I protested.

"And that we did. The grief that we experienced when we understood how we had so wasted our lives was beyond any grief possible on earth. The darkness of that grief can only be understood by those who have experienced it. Such darkness is magnified when it is revealed next to the glory of the One we failed.

"You are standing among those in the lowest rank of heaven. There is no greater folly than to know the great salvation of God, but to then go on living for yourself. To come here and learn the reality of that is a grief beyond what an earthly soul can experience. We are those who suffered outer darkness because of this greatest of follies."

I was still incredulous. "But you are more glorious and full of joy and peace than I even imagined, even for those in heaven. I do not sense any remorse in you, and yet I know that here you cannot lie. This does not make sense to me."

Looking me straight in the eyes, he continued, "The Lord also loves us with a love greater than you can yet understand. Before His judgment seat I tasted the greatest remorse and darkness of soul that can be experienced. Though here we do not measure time as you do, it seemed to last for as long as my life on earth had lasted. All my sins and follies that I had not repented of passed before me, and before all who are here.

"You cannot understand the grief of this until you have experienced it," he went on. "I felt that I was in the deepest dungeon of hell, even as I stood before the glory of the Lord. He was resolute until my life had been completely reviewed. When I said I was sorry and asked for the mercy of His cross,

He wiped away my tears and took away the darkness. I no longer feel the bitterness that I knew as I stood before Him, but I remember it.

"Here you can remember such things without continuing to feel the pain. A moment in the lowest part of heaven is much greater than a thousand years of the highest life on earth. Now my mourning at my folly has been turned into joy, and I know that I will experience joy forever, even if I am in the lowest place in heaven."

I began to think again of the treasures of salvation. Somehow I knew that all this man had told me was revealed by those treasures. Every step I had taken up the mountain, or into it, had revealed that His ways are both more fearful and more wonderful than I had ever been able to comprehend before.

Looking at me intently, my former acquaintance continued: "You are not here just to gain understanding, but to be changed. The next level of rank has glory many times greater than what we have here. Each new level is that much greater than the previous one. It is not just that those on each level have an even more glorious spiritual body, but that each level is closer to the throne, from where all the glory comes.

"Even so, I no longer feel the grief of my failure. I really deserve nothing. I am here by grace alone, and I am so thankful for what I have. He is so worthy to be loved. I could be doing many wondrous things now in the different realms of heaven, but I would rather stay here and just behold His glory, even if I am on the outer fringes."

Then, with a distant look in his eyes, he added, "Everyone in heaven is now in this room to watch His great mystery unfold, and to watch those of you who will fight the last battle."

"Can you see Him from here?" I asked. "I see His glory far away, but I cannot see Him."

"I can see many times better than you can," he answered. "And yes, I can see Him and hear Him. I can see all that He is doing. He also gave us power to observe what is happening on earth. We are the great cloud of witnesses who are watching you and cheering you on."

He bowed, and then returned to the ranks. I began walking again, trying to understand all that he had said to me. As I looked over the great host that he said were the foolish virgins, the ones who had spiritually slept away their lives on earth, I knew that if any one of them appeared on earth now they would be worshiped as gods. Yet, they were the very least of those who were here!

I then began to think of all of the time that I had wasted in my own life. It was such an overwhelming thought that I stopped. Then parts of my life began to pass before me. I began to experience a terrible grief over my sin. I, too, had been one of the greatest of fools! I may have kept more oil in my lamp than others, but now I knew how foolish I had been to measure what was required of me by how others were doing. I, too, was one of the foolish virgins!

The Would-Be Mentor

Just when I thought I would collapse under the weight of this terrible discovery, a man I had known and esteemed as a great man of God came forward to steady me. As he greeted me warmly, his touch somehow revived me.

I had wanted to be discipled by this man, but we did not get along well. As had happened with a number of other men of God I tried to get close to, I was an irritation to this man, and he had finally asked me to leave. For years I had felt guilty about this, convinced that I had missed a great opportunity because of some flaw in my character. Even though I had put it out of my mind, I still carried the weight of this failure. When I saw him it all surfaced, and a sick feeling came over me. Now he was so regal that I felt even more repulsive and embarrassed by my poor condition. I wanted to hide, but there was no way I could avoid him here.

To my surprise, his warmth toward me was so genuine that he soon put me at ease. There did not seem to be any barriers between us. In fact, the love I felt coming from him almost completely took away my self-consciousness.

"I have waited eagerly for this meeting," he said.

"You were waiting for me?" I asked. "Why?"

"You are just one of many that I am waiting for. I did not understand until my judgment that you were one that I was called to help—to even disciple—but I rejected you."

"Sir," I protested, "it would have been a great honor to have been discipled by you, and I am very thankful for the time I did have with you. But I was so arrogant that I deserved the rejection. I know that my rebellion and pride have prevented me from having a real spiritual father. This was not your fault, but mine."

"It is true that you were prideful, but that is not why I was offended with you," he said. "I was offended because of my insecurity, which made me want to control everyone around me. I was offended that you would not accept everything I said without questioning it. I then started to look for anything that was wrong with you so I could justify rejecting you. I began to feel that if I could not control you, one day you would embarrass me and my ministry. I esteemed my ministry more than I did the people for whom it was given to me, so I drove you and many others like you away."

"I must admit that at times I thought you had turned into a . . ." I stopped myself, embarrassed by what I was about to say.

"And you were right," he said with a genuineness that is unknown in the realms of earth. "I had been given the grace to be a spiritual father, but I was a very poor one. All children are rebellious. They are all self-centered, and think the world revolves around them. That is why they need parents to raise them. Almost every child will at times bring reproach on his family, but he is still a part of the family.

"I turned away many of God's own children—precious people He had entrusted to me so they could be brought to maturity. I failed with many of those who stayed with me. Most of them suffered terrible and unnecessary wounds and failures that I could have helped them avoid. Many of them are now prisoners of the enemy.

"I built a large organization," he continued, "and had considerable influence in the church. But the greatest gifts the Lord entrusted to me were the people who were sent to me for discipling, many of whom I rejected. Had I not been so self-centered and concerned with my own reputation, I would be a king here. I was called to sit on one of the highest thrones. All that you have and will accomplish would have been in my heavenly account as well. Instead, much of what I gave my attention to was of very little eternal significance."

"What you accomplished was astounding," I interjected.

"What looks good on earth looks very different here. What will make you a king on earth will often be a stumbling block to keep you from being a king here. What will make you a king here is lowly and unacclaimed on earth. I failed some of the greatest tests and greatest opportunities that were given to me, one of which was you. Will you forgive me?"

"Of course," I said, embarrassed. "But I am in need of your forgiveness, too. I still think that it was my awkwardness and rebellion that made it difficult for you. In fact, I too have failed to let some people get close to me who wanted to—for the same reasons you did not want me around you."

"It is true that you were not perfect," he replied, "and I discerned some of your problems rightly. Yet that is never reason to reject someone. The Lord did not reject the world when He saw its failures. He did not reject me when He saw my sin. He laid down His life for me. It is always the greater who must lay down his life for the lesser. Even though I was more mature and had more authority than you, I became like one of the goats in the parable, rejecting the Lord by rejecting you and many others He sent to me."

As he talked, his words were striking me deeply. I, too, was guilty of everything he mentioned. Passing through my mind were the faces of many young men and women I had brushed off as not being important enough for my time. I desperately wanted to return and gather them together!

The grief that I began to feel was even worse than I had felt about wasting my time. I had wasted *people*! Now many of these were prisoners of the enemy, wounded and captured during the battle on the mountain. This whole battle was for the people, and yet people are often our least concern. We will fight for truths more than for the people for whom the truths are given. We will fight for ministries, while running roughshod over the people in them.

"And many people think of me as a spiritual leader! I am truly the least of the saints," I thought out loud.

The Enemy of the Gospel

"I understand how you feel," remarked another man. I recognized him as someone I considered one of the greatest Christian leaders of all time. "Near the end of his life, Paul the apostle said he was the least of the saints. Then, just before his death, he even called himself 'the greatest of sinners.' If he hadn't learned that lesson during his life on earth, he, too, would have been in jeopardy of becoming one of the least of the saints in heaven. Because he learned it on earth, he is now one of those closest to the Lord, and will be one of the highest in rank for all of eternity."

Seeing this man in the company of "the foolish virgins" was the greatest surprise I had yet. "I cannot believe that you, too, are one of the foolish who slept away their lives on earth. Why are you here?"

"I am here because I made one of the gravest mistakes you can make as one entrusted with the glorious gospel of our Savior," he answered. "Just as the apostle Paul progressed from not considering himself inferior to the greatest apostles, to being the greatest of sinners, I took the opposite course. I started out knowing that I had been one of the greatest of sinners who had found grace, but ended up thinking I was one of the greatest apostles. It was because of my great pride, not insecurity like our friend here, that I began to attack everyone who did not see everything just the way I did.

"I stripped those who followed me of their own callings and even their personalities, pressuring them to all become just like me. No one around me could be himself. No one dared to question me, because they knew I would crush them into powder. I thought that by making others smaller I made myself greater. I thought that I was supposed to be the Holy Spirit to everyone.

"From the outside my ministry looked like a smooth running machine where everyone was in unity and there was perfect order—but it was the order of a concentration camp. I took the Lord's children and made them automatons. I molded them into my own image instead of His. In the end I was not even serving the Lord, but rather the idol I had built to myself. By the end of my life I was actually an enemy of the true gospel, at least in practice, even if my teachings and writings seemed impeccably biblical."

Coming from this person, such statements astounded me. I began to wonder if every meeting I had here was meant to give me a greater shock than the previous one.

"If it is true that you became an enemy of the gospel, how is it that you are still here?" I questioned.

"By the grace of God, I did trust in the cross for my own salvation. However, I actually kept other men from it, leading them to myself rather than to the Lord. Even so, the blessed Savior remains faithful to us even when we are unfaithful. It was also by His grace that the Lord took me from the earth sooner than He would have, just so those who were under me could find Him and come to know Him."

Through a Glass Darkly

I could not have been more stunned to think that this particular man was guilty of such things. History had given us a very different picture of him.

Reading what was going on in my heart, he continued: "God does have a different set of history books than those on the earth. You have had a glimpse of this, but you do not yet know *how* different they are. Earthly histories will pass away, but the books that are kept here will last forever. If you can rejoice in what heaven is recording about your life, you are blessed indeed. Men see through a glass darkly, so their histories will always be clouded, and sometimes completely wrong."

"How was it that so many other leaders esteemed you so?" I inquired, still having trouble absorbing what I was hearing.

"Very few Christians, even very few leaders, have the true gift of discernment. Without this gift it is impossible to accurately discern truth in those of the present or the past. Even with this gift it is difficult. Until we have been here and been stripped, we will judge others through distorted prejudices, either positive or negative. That is why we were warned not to judge before the time.

"Until we have been here, we cannot really know what is in the heart of others and whether they are performing good or evil deeds. There have been good motives in even the worst of men, and evil motives in even the best of them. Only here can men be judged by both their deeds and their motives."

"When I return to earth, will I be able to discern history accurately because I have been here?"

"You are here because you prayed for the Lord to judge you severely, to correct you ruthlessly, so that you could serve Him more perfectly. This was one of the wisest requests you have ever made. The wise judge themselves lest they be judged. The even wiser ask for the judgments of the Lord, because they realize that they cannot even judge themselves well.

"Having come here, you will leave with far more wisdom and discernment, but on earth you will always see through a glass darkly at least to some degree. Although your experience here will help you to know men better, only when you are fully here can you know them fully. When you leave here you will be more impressed by how *little* you know men rather than by how well you know them. This is just as true in relation to the histories of men. I have been allowed to talk with you because I have in a sense discipled you through my writings, and you will be helped by knowing the truth about me," the famous Reformer concluded.

The Reformer's Wife

Then a woman I did not know stepped forward. Her beauty and grace were breathtaking, but it was not sensual or seductive in any way.

"I was his wife on earth," she began. "Much of what you know of him actually came from me. Therefore, what I am about to say is not just about him, but about us. You can reform the church without reforming your own soul. You can dictate the course of history, and yet not do the Father's will or glorify His Son. If you commit yourself to making human history, you may do it—but it is a fleeting accomplishment that will evaporate like a wisp of smoke."

"But your husband's work, or your work, greatly impacted every generation after him for good. It is hard to imagine how dark the world would have been without him," I protested.

"True," she answered. "But you can gain the whole world and still lose your own soul. Only if you keep your own soul pure can you truly impact the world for the eternal purposes of God. My husband lost his soul to me, and he only regained it at the end of his life because I was taken from the earth so that he could.

"Much of what my husband did, he did more for me than for the Lord. I pressured him and even gave him much of the knowledge that he taught. I used him as an extension of my own ego, because as a woman at the time I could not be recognized as a spiritual leader myself. In a sense, I took over his life, so that I could live my life through him. Soon I had him doing everything just to prove himself to me."

"You must have loved her very much," I said, looking at him.

"No, I did not love her at all," he said to my amazement. "Neither did she love me. In fact, after just a few years of marriage we did not even like each other. But we both needed each other, so we found a way to work together. Our marriage was not a yoke of love, but of bondage. The more successful we became, the more unhappy we became, and the more deception we used to fool those who followed us. We were empty wretches by the end of our lives.

"The more influence that you gain by your own self-promotion, the more you must strive to retain your influence, and the more your life will become dark and cruel. Kings feared us, but we feared everyone, from the kings to the peasants. We could trust no one, because we were living in such deception ourselves that we did not even trust each other. We preached love and trust, because we wanted everyone to love and trust us. But we, ourselves, secretly feared and despised everyone. If you preach the greatest truths but do not live them, you are only the greatest hypocrite and the most tormented soul."

Their words pounded me like a hammer. I could see that my life was already heading in the same direction. How much was I doing to promote myself rather than Christ? I began to see how much I did just to prove myself to others, especially those I felt in competition with or those who disliked or rejected me. I began to see how much of my own life was built on the facade of a projected image that belied who I really was. But here I could not hide. This great cloud of witnesses all knew who I was beyond the veil of my projected motives.

I looked again at this couple. They were now so guile-less and so noble that it was impossible to question their motives. They were gladly exposing their most devious sins for my sake, and were genuinely happy to be able to do it.

"I may have had a wrong concept of you by your history and your writings, but I have even more esteem for you now," I told them. "I pray that I can carry from this place the integrity and freedom that you now have. I am tired of trying to live up to projected images of myself. How I long for that freedom!" I lamented, wanting desperately to remember every detail of this encounter.

The High Calling

Then the famous Reformer offered a final exhortation: "Do not try to teach others to do what you, yourself, are not doing. Reformation is not just a doctrine. True reformation only comes from union with the Savior. When you are yoked with Christ, carrying the burdens that He gives you, He will be with you and carry them for you. You can only do His work when you are doing it *with* Him, not just *for* Him.

"Only the Spirit can beget that which is Spirit. If you are truly yoked with Him, you will do nothing for the sake of politics or history. Anything you do because of political pressures or opportunities will only lead you to the end of your true ministry. The things that are done in an effort to make history will at best confine your accomplishments to history, and you will fail to impact eternity. If you do not live what you preach to others, you disqualify yourself from the high calling of God, just as we did."

"I do not think I could even consider seeking a high calling," I interrupted. "I don't even deserve to sit here in this place you say is for the *lowest* rank in heaven. How could I ever consider seeking a high calling?"

"The high calling is not out of reach for anyone that the Lord has called. I will tell you what will keep you on the path of life—love the Savior and seek His glory alone. Everything you do to exalt yourself will one day bring you the most terrible humiliation. Everything you do out of genuine love for the Savior, to glorify His name, will extend the limits of His eternal kingdom and ultimately result in a much higher place for yourself. Live for what is recorded here. Care nothing for what is recorded on earth."

The couple then parted with a cheerful embrace, yet I felt anything but cheerful. As they walked away, I was again overwhelmed by my own sin. Memories of the times I had used people for my own purposes, or even used the name of Jesus to further my own ambitions or make myself look better, began to cascade down upon me. Here, in this place where I could behold the power and glory of the One I had so used, such memories became more repulsive than I could stand. I fell on my face in the worst despair I had ever known.

After what seemed like an eternity of seeing people and events pass before me, I felt the Reformer's wife lifting me to my feet again. I was overcome by her purity, especially as I now felt so evil and corrupt. I had the strongest desire to worship her because she was so pure.

"Turn to the Son," she said emphatically. "Your desire to worship me, or anyone else at this time, is only an attempt to turn the attention away from yourself, and justify yourself by serving what you are not. I am pure now because I turned to Him. You need to see the corruption that is in your own soul, but then you must not dwell on yourself or seek to justify yourself with dead works, but turn to Him."

She said this with such genuine love that it was impossible to be hurt or offended by it. When she saw that I understood, she continued:

"The purity you saw in me was what my husband first saw in me when we were young. I was relatively pure in my motives then, but I corrupted his love and my own purity by allowing him to worship me wrongly. You can never become pure by worshiping those who are more pure than yourself. You must go beyond them to find the One who has *made them* pure, and in Whom alone there is no sin.

"The more people praised us, and the more we accepted their praises, the further we drifted from the path of life. Then we started living for the praises of men, and to gain power over those who would not praise us. That was our demise, and it was the same for many who are here in the lowest place."

Purified Love

Simply wanting to prolong our conversation, I asked the next question that came to my mind, "Is it difficult for you and your husband to be here together?"

"Not at all," she responded. "All the relationships you have on earth are continued here. They are all purified by the judgment and by the fact that they are now spiritual, just as we are now spirit. The more you are forgiven, the more you love. After we forgave each other, we loved each other more. Now our relationship is continuing in much greater depth and richness, because we are joint heirs of this salvation.

"As deep as the wounds were that we afflicted upon each other, that is how deep the love was able to reach when we were healed. We could have experienced this on earth, but we did not learn forgiveness in time. If we had learned forgiveness, the competition that entered our relationship and sidetracked our lives would not have been able to take root in us. If you truly love, you will truly forgive. The harder it is for you to forgive, the further you are from true love. Forgiveness is essential, or you will stumble and stray from the course chosen for you."

I realized that this woman, who had brought me into such confrontation with the pain of my own depravity, was also the most attractive person I could ever remember meeting. It was not romantic attraction, but I just did not want to leave her. Perceiving my thoughts, she withdrew a step, indicating that she was about to go. But before leaving, she offered me some final insights.

"The pure truth, spoken in pure love, will always attract," she said. "You will remember the pain you feel here, and it will help you through the rest of your life. Pain is good; it shows you where there is a problem. Do not try to reduce the pain until you find the problem. God's truth often brings pain as it highlights a problem that we have, but His truth will always show us the way to freedom, too. When you know this, you will even begin to rejoice in your trials, which are all allowed to help keep you on the path of life.

"Your attraction to me is not out of order. It is the attraction between male and female that was given in the beginning, which is pure in its original form. When pure truth is combined with pure love, men can be the men they were created to be without having to dominate women out of insecurity. Such domination is nothing but lust, which is the lowest depth to which love falls because of our sin. With true love, men become true men. Women, likewise, can be the women they were created to be, because their love has replaced their fear.

"Love will never manipulate or try to control out of insecurity, because love casts out all fear. The very place where relationships can be the most corrupted is also where they can be the most fulfilling, after redemption has worked in them. True love is a taste of heaven, and lust is the enemy's ultimate perversion of the glory of heaven. To the degree that you are free of lust on earth, you will begin to experience heaven."

"But I do not think I have felt any lust for you, or for *anyone* while I've been here," I mildly protested. "On the contrary, I was marveling that I could behold one with your beauty and not feel lust."

"That is because you are here. The light of His glory here casts out all darkness. But if you were not here, lust would be gripping you now," she said.

"I'm sure you are right. Can we ever be free from this terrible perversion on earth?" I begged.

"Yes. As your mind is renewed by the Spirit of Truth, you will not see relationships as opportunities to *take* from others, but to give. Giving provides the greatest fulfillment that we can ever know. The most wonderful human relationships are but fleeting glimpses of the ecstasy that comes when we give ourselves to the Lord in pure worship. What we experience in worship here your frail, unglorified body could not endure. The true worship of God will purify the soul for the glory of true relationships.

"Therefore, you must not seek relationships, but true worship. Only then can relationships start to be what they are supposed to be. True love never seeks to be first, or to be in control, but rather it takes the place of humble service. If my husband and I had kept this in our marriage, we would be sitting next to the King now, and this great hall would be filled with many more souls."

Removing More Veils

With that, the Reformer's wife disappeared back into the ranks of the glorified saints. I looked again toward the throne and was taken aback because the glory appeared so much more beautiful than it had before. Another man standing close to me explained:

"With each encounter, a veil is being removed so that you can see Him more clearly. You are not changed just by seeing His glory, but by seeing it with an unveiled face. Those who come to the true judgments of God walk a corridor such as this to meet those who can help them remove whatever veils they are still wearing, veils that will distort their vision of Him."

I felt that I had already absorbed more understanding than my many years of ministry on earth had given me. All my study and seeking on earth had apparently only lead me forward at a snail's pace. Even *many* lifetimes would not have prepared me to face the judgement! My life had already disqualified me more than all those I had met, and it seemed they had barely made it here!

"How could those who have not been given the grace of this experience have any hope at all?" I asked.

I heard a new voice say, "What you are experiencing here has been given you on earth. Every relationship, every encounter with another person, could teach you what you are learning here if you keep that cloak of humility on and learn to always keep your attention fixed on His glory. You are being given this experience now because you will write the vision, and those who read it will understand it. Many will then be able to carry the glory and the power that they will need in the last battle."

I was amazed to recognize this man as a contemporary of mine, for I did not even know he had died. I had never met him on earth, but he had a great ministry which I respected very much. Through men that he had trained, thousands had been led to salvation, and many large churches had been raised up that were almost totally devoted to evangelism.

He asked if he could just embrace me for a minute, and I agreed, feeling quite awkward. When we embraced, I felt such love coming from him that a great pain deep within me stopped hurting. I had become so used to the pain that I did not even notice it until it stopped. After he released me, I told him that his embrace had healed me of something. His joy at this was profound. Then he began to tell me why he was in the lowest rank in heaven.

"I became so proud near the end of my life that I could not imagine that the Lord would do anything of significance unless He did it through me. I began to touch the Lord's anointed, and to do His prophets harm. I was selfishly proud when the Lord used one of my own disciples, and I became jealous when the Lord moved through anyone who was outside of my own ministry. I would search for anything that was wrong with them in order to expose them. I did not know that every time I did this I only demoted myself further."

"I never knew that you had done anything like that," I said, surprised.

"I did not do it myself, but I incited men under me to investigate other ministers and do my dirty work. I had them scour the earth to find any error or sin in the life of others so they could be exposed. I became the worst thing that a man can become on the earth—a stumbling block who produced other stumbling blocks. We sowed fear and division throughout the church, all in the name of protecting the truth. In my self-righteousness, I was headed for perdition.

"But in His great mercy, the Lord allowed me to be struck by a disease that would bring about a slow and humiliating death. Just before I died, I came to my senses and repented. I am thankful to be here at all. I may be one of the least of His here, but it is much more than I deserve. I just could not leave this room until I had a chance to apologize to those of you that I so wronged."

"But you never wronged me," I said.

"Oh, but I did indeed," he replied. "Many of the attacks that came against you were from those I had agitated and encouraged in their assaults on others. Even though I may not have personally carried out the attacks, the Lord holds me as responsible as those who did."

"I see. Of course I forgive you."

Judging the Stumbling Blocks

I was already beginning to remember how I had done this same thing, even though on a smaller scale. I recalled how I had allowed disgruntled former members of a nearby church to spread their poison about that church without stopping them. By allowing them to do this without correcting them, I had, in effect, encouraged them to continue. At the time I had rationalized that this was justified because of the errors of that church. I had even repeated many of their stories, justifying it under the guise of enlisting prayers for them.

Soon a great flood of memories of other such incidents began to arise in my heart. Again, I was starting to be overwhelmed by the evil and darkness of my own soul.

"I, too, have been a stumbling block!" I wailed. I knew that I deserved death and that I deserved the worst kind of hell. I had never seen such ruthlessness and cruelty as I was now seeing in my own heart.

"We actually comforted ourselves by thinking we were doing God a favor when we attacked His children," continued the understanding voice of this man. "It is good for you to see this here, because you can go back. Please warn my disciples of their impending doom if they do not repent. Many of them are called to be kings here, but if they do not repent they will face the worst judgment of all—the judgment of the stumbling blocks.

"My humbling disease was grace from God. When I stood before the throne, I asked the Lord to send such grace to my disciples. I cannot cross back over to them, but He has allowed me this time with you. Please forgive and release those who have attacked you. They really do not understand that they are doing the work of the Accuser. Thank you for forgiving me, but please also forgive them. It is in your power to retain sins or to cover them with love. I entreat you to love those who are now your enemies."

I was so overwhelmed with my own sin that I could hardly hear this man. He was glorious and pure, and obviously now had powers that were not known on the earth. Yet, he was entreating me with a great humility. I felt such love coming from him that I could not imagine refusing him. But even without the impact of his love, I felt far more guilty than anyone attacking me could possibly be.

"Certainly I must deserve anything they have done to me, and much more," I replied.

"That is true, but it is not the point here," he entreated. "Everyone on earth is deserving of the second death, but our Savior brought us grace and truth. If we are to do His work, we must do everything in both grace and truth. Truth without grace is what the enemy brings when he comes as an 'angel of light.'"

"If I can be delivered from this, maybe I will be able to help them," I replied. "But can't you recognize that I am far worse than they could possibly be?"

"I know that what just passed through your memory was bad," he answered, with profound love and grace. I knew that he had now become as concerned for me and my condition as he had been for his own disciples.

"This really is heaven," I blurted out. "This really is light and truth. How could we who live in such darkness become so proud, thinking we know so much about God?" Impulsively, I yelled in the direction of the throne, "Lord! Please let me go and carry this light back to earth!"

Immediately the entire host of heaven seemed to stand at attention, and I knew that I was the center of their gaze. I felt so insignificant before just one of these glorious ones, but when I knew they were *all* looking at me, fear came like a tidal wave. I felt that there could be no doom like I was about to experience. Surely I was the greatest enemy of the glory and truth that so filled that place.

When I thought about my request to go back, I realized I was too depraved. I could never adequately represent such glory and truth. There was no way that I could, in my corruption, convey the reality of that glorious place and Presence. I felt that even Satan had not fallen as far as I had. *This is hell!* I thought. There could be no worse pain than to be as evil as I was and to know that this kind of glory exists. To be banned from here would be a torture worse than I ever feared. "No wonder the demons are so angry and demented," I said under my breath.

Just when I felt that I was about to be banished to the deepest regions of hell, I simply cried, "JESUS!" Immediately, a deep peace came over me. I knew I had to move on toward the glory again, and somehow I had the confidence to do it.

The Writer's Remorse

I kept moving until I saw a man I considered to be one of the greatest writers of all time. I had counted his insights into the truth to be possibly the greatest I had encountered in all my studies.

"Sir, I have always looked forward to this meeting," I blurted out.

"As have I," he replied with genuine sincerity.

I was surprised by his comment, but I was so excited to meet him that I continued, "I feel that I know you, and in your writings I felt like you somehow knew me. I think I owe more to you than to anyone else who was not canonized in Scripture."

"You are very gracious," he replied. "But I am sorry that I did not serve you better. I was a shallow person, and my writings were shallow, filled more with worldly wisdom than divine truth."

"I know that what you are saying must be true, because you can only speak the truth here," I told him. "Yet it is hard for me to understand. I think your writings are some of the best that we have on earth."

"You are right," this famous writer admitted with sincerity. "It is so sad. Everyone here, even those who sit closest to the King, would live their lives differently if they had them to live over. But I think I would live mine even more differently than most. I was honored by kings, but failed the King of Kings. I used the great gifts and insights that were given to me to draw men more to myself and my wisdom than to Him. Besides, I only knew Him by the hearing of the ear, which is the way I compelled other men to know Him. I made them dependent on me, and on others like me. I turned them more to deductive reasoning than to the Holy Spirit, Whom I hardly knew.

"I did not point men to Jesus," he continued, "but to myself and others like me who pretended to know Him. When I beheld Him here, I wanted to grind my writings into powder, just as Moses did to the golden calf. My mind was my idol, and I wanted everyone to worship my mind with me.

"Your esteem for me does not cause me to rejoice. If I had spent as much time seeking to know Him as I did seeking to know *about* Him in order to impress others with my knowledge, many of those who are in this lowest of companies would be sitting in the thrones that were prepared for them. And many others would be in this room."

"I know that what you are saying about your work must be true, but aren't you being a little too hard on yourself?"

I questioned. "Your works fed me spiritually for many years, as I know they have multitudes of others."

"I am not being too hard on myself," he responded. "All that I have said is true, and it was confirmed when I stood before the throne. Even though I produced a lot, I was given more talents than almost anyone here, and I buried them beneath my own spiritual pride and ambitions. Just as we learn from the example of Adam—who could have carried the whole human race into a most glorious future, but by his failure led billions of souls into the worst of dooms instead—with authority comes responsibility.

"The more authority you are given, the more potential for both good and evil you have. Those who will rule with Him for the ages will know responsibility of the most profound kind. No man stands alone, and every human failure or victory resonates far beyond our comprehension, even to generations to come."

I couldn't help reflecting on the beautiful and articulate phrases that this man had written. He was the epitome of a wordsmith, a craftsman who turned words into works of art. But here, he was speaking as a common man, without the flair for which his writings were so well known. Although he knew what I was thinking, as did everyone here, he continued with what he clearly thought was more important.

"Had I sought the Lord Himself instead of knowledge about Him, I could have successfully led many thousands, which would have resulted in many more millions being here now. Anyone who understands the true nature of authority would never seek it. They would only accept it when they knew they were yoked with the Lord, the only One who can carry authority without stumbling. Never seek influence for yourself, but only seek the Lord and be willing to take His yoke. My influence did not feed your heart, but rather your pride in knowledge."

"How can I know that I am not doing the same?" I asked as I began to think of my own writings.

"Study to show yourself approved unto God, not men," he replied as he walked back into the ranks. Before disappearing he turned, and with the slightest smile offered one last bit of advice: "And do not follow me."

Higher Ranks

In this first multitude I saw many other men and women of God, both from history and from my own time. I stopped and talked to many of them, and was shocked that so many I expected to be in the highest positions were instead in the lowest rank of the kingdom. Many shared the same basic story—they had fallen to the deadly sin of pride after their great victories, or fallen to jealousy when other men were anointed as much as they were. Others had fallen

141

to lust, discouragement or bitterness near the end of their lives, and had to be taken before they crossed the line into perdition. They all gave me the same warning: the higher the spiritual authority that you walk in, the further you can fall if you are without love and humility.

As I continued toward the judgment seat, I began to pass those who were of higher rank in the kingdom. After many more veils had been stripped away from me by meetings with those who had stumbled over the same problems that I had, I began to meet some who had overcome. I met couples who had served God and each other faithfully to the end. Their glory here was unspeakable, and their victory encouraged me that it was possible to stay on the path of life and serve the Lord faithfully.

Those who stumbled did so in many different ways. But those who prevailed all did it the same way: They did not deviate from their devotion to the first and greatest commandment—loving the Lord. In this way, their service was done unto Him, not to men. These were the ones who worshiped the Lamb and followed Him wherever He went.

When I was still not even halfway to the throne, what had been the indescribable glory of the first rank now seemed to be outer darkness in comparison to the glory of those I was now passing. The greatest beauty on earth would not qualify to be found anywhere in heaven. And I was told that this room was just the *threshold* of indescribable realms of glory!

My march to the throne may have taken days, months or even years. There was no way to measure time in that place. Everyone there showed respect to me, not because of who I was or anything I had done, but simply because I was a warrior in the battle of the last days. Somehow, through this last battle, the glory of God was to be revealed in such a way that it would be a witness to every power and authority, created or yet to be created, for all of eternity. During this battle the glory of the cross would be revealed, and the wisdom of God would be known in a special way. To be in that battle was to be given one of the greatest honors possible.

Near the judgment seat of Christ, those in the highest ranks were sitting on thrones that were all a part of His throne. Even the least of these thrones was many times more glorious than any earthly throne. Some of those on the thrones were rulers over cities on earth, and would soon take their places. Others were rulers over the affairs of heaven, and still others ruled over the affairs of the physical creation, such as star systems and galaxies.

It was apparent that those who were given authority over cities were esteemed even above those who had been given authority over galaxies. The value of a single child surpasses that of a galaxy of stars, because the Lord has chosen men as His eternal dwelling place. In the presence of His glory, the whole earth seemed as insignificant as a speck of dust. Yet, it was so infinitely esteemed that the attention of the whole creation was upon it.

His Awesome Presence

Now that I stood before the throne, I felt even lower than a speck of dust. Nevertheless, I felt the Holy Spirit upon me in a greater way than I ever had. It was by His power alone that I was able to stand. It was here that I truly came to understand His ministry as the Comforter. He had led me through the entire journey, even though for the most part I had been unaware of His presence.

The Lord was both more gentle and more terrible than I had ever imagined. In Him I saw Wisdom, who had accompanied me on the mountain. I somehow also felt the familiarity of many of my friends on earth, which I understood to be because He had often spoken to me through them. I also recognized Him as the One I had often rejected when He had come to me in others. I saw both a Lion and a Lamb, the Shepherd and the Bridegroom, but most of all I now saw Him as the Judge.

Even in the Lord's awesome presence, the Comforter was so mightily with me that I was comfortable. It was clear that the Lord in no way wanted me to be uncomfortable; He only wanted me to know the truth. Human words are not adequate to describe either how awesome or how relieving it was to stand before Him. I had passed the point where I was concerned if the judgment was going to be good or bad; I just knew it would be right, and that I could trust my Judge.

At one point the Lord looked toward the galleries of thrones around Him. Many were occupied, but many were empty. He then said, *"These thrones are for the overcomers who have served Me faithfully in every generation. My Father and I prepared them before the foundation of the world. Are you worthy to sit on one of these?"*

I remembered what a friend had once said, "When the omniscient God asks you a question, it is not because He is seeking information." I looked at those who were now seated on the thrones. I could recognize some of the great heroes of the faith, but realized most of those seated had not even been well known on earth.

Many of those on the thrones had been missionaries who expended their lives in obscurity. They had never cared to be remembered on earth, but wanted only to be remembered by Him. I was a bit surprised to see some who had been wealthy, and rulers who had been faithful with what they had been given. However, it seemed that faithful, praying women and mothers occupied more thrones than any other single group.

There was no way I could answer "yes" to the Lord's question regarding whether I considered myself worthy to sit here. I was not worthy to sit in the company of any who were there. I knew I had been given the opportunity to run for the greatest prize in heaven or earth, and I had failed. I was desperate, but there was still one hope. Even though most of my life had been a failure, I was very glad that I was here before finishing my life on earth.

When I confessed that I was not worthy, the Lord asked, *"But do you want this seat?"*

"I do with all of my heart," I responded.

The Lord then looked at the galleries and said, *"Those empty seats could have been filled in any generation. I gave the invitation to sit here to everyone who has called upon My name. The seats are still available. Now the last battle has come, and many who are last shall be first. These seats will be filled before the battle is over. Those who will sit here will be known by two things: they will wear the mantle of humility, and they will have My likeness.*

"You now have the mantle. If you can keep it and do not lose it in the battle, when you return you will also have My likeness. Then you will be worthy to sit with these, because I will have made you worthy. All authority and power has been given to Me, and I alone can wield it. You will prevail, and you will be trusted with My authority only when you have come to fully abide in Me. Now turn and look at My household."

I turned and looked back in the direction I had come from. Standing before His throne, I could see the entire room. The spectacle was glorious beyond description. Millions filled the ranks. Each individual in the lowest rank was more awesome than any army, and had more power. It was far beyond my capacity to absorb such a panorama of glory. Even so, I could see that only a very small portion of the great room was occupied.

The Cup of Tears

I then looked back at the Lord and was astonished to see tears in His eyes. He had wiped the tears away from every eye here, except His own. As a tear ran down His cheek, He caught it in His hand. He then offered it to me.

"This is My cup. Will you drink it with Me?"

There was no way that I could refuse Him. As the Lord continued to look at me, I began to feel His great love. Even as foul as I was, He still loved me. As undeserving as I was, He wanted me to be close to Him. Then He said:

"I love all of these with a love that you cannot now understand. I also love all who are supposed to be here but did not come. I left the ninety-nine to go after the one who was lost. My shepherds would not leave the one to go after the ninety-nine who are still lost. I came to save the lost. Will you share My heart to go and save the lost? Will you help to fill this room? Will you help to fill these thrones, and every other seat in this hall? Will you take up this quest to bring joy to heaven, to Me and to My Father?

147

"This is judgment for My own household, and My own house is not full. The last battle will not be over until My house is full. Only then will it be time for us to redeem the earth and remove the evil from My creation. If you drink My cup, you will love the lost the way that I love them."

He took a cup so plain that it seemed out of place in a room of such glory, and He placed His tear in it. He then gave it to me. I have never tasted anything so bitter! I knew that I could in no way drink it all, or even much of it, but I was determined to drink as much as I could. The Lord patiently waited until I finally erupted into such weeping that I felt like rivers of tears were flowing from me. I was crying for the lost, but even more I was crying for the Lord.

I looked to Him in desperation, for I could not take any more of the great pain. Then His peace began to fill me, flowing together with the river of His love that erupted when I drank from His cup. Never had I felt anything so wonderful. This was the living water that I knew would spring up for eternity.

Then I felt as if the waters flowing within me caught on fire! I began to feel that this fire would consume me if I could not start declaring the majesty of His glory. I had never felt such an urge to preach, to worship Him, and to breathe every breath for the sake of His gospel.

"Lord!" I shouted, forgetting everyone but Him. "I now know that this throne of judgment is also the throne of grace, and I ask You now for the grace to serve You. Above all things, I ask You for grace! I ask You for the grace to finish my course. I ask You for the grace to love You like this, so I can be delivered from the delusions and self-centeredness that have so perverted my life.

"I call upon You for salvation from myself and the evil of my heart, so this love I now feel can flow in my heart continually. I ask You to give me Your heart, Your love. I ask for the grace of the Holy Spirit to convict me of my sin and to testify of You as You really are. Give me the grace to preach the reality of this judgment and testify of all You have prepared for those who come to You. I ask for the grace to share with those who are called to occupy these empty thrones, to give them words of encouragement that will keep them on the path of life and impart to them the faith to do what they have been called to do. Lord, I beg You for this grace!"

Commissioned

The Lord then stood up, and all those who were seated upon the thrones for as far as I could see also stood up. His eyes burned with a fire I had not seen before.

"You have called upon Me for grace. This request I never deny. You shall return, and the Holy Spirit shall be with you. Here

you have tasted of both My kindness and My severity. You must remember both if you are to stay on the path of life. The true love of God includes the judgment of God. You must know both my kindness and severity or you will fall to deception. This is the grace that you have been given here, to know both. The conversations you had with your brethren here were My grace. Remember them."

He pointed His sword toward my heart, then my mouth, then my hands. When He did, fire came from His sword and burned me. The pain was very great. *"This, too, is grace,"* He said. *"You are but one of many who have been prepared for this hour. Preach and write about all that you have seen here. What I have said to you, say to My brethren.*

"Go and call My captains to the last battle. Go and defend the poor and the oppressed, the widows and the orphans. This is the commission of My captains, and it is where you will find them. My children are worth more to Me than the stars in the heavens. Feed My lambs. Watch over My little ones. Give the word of God to them that they may live. Go to the battle. Go and do not retreat. Go quickly, for I will come quickly. Obey Me and hasten the day of My coming."

A company of angels then came and escorted me away from the throne. The leader walked beside me and began to speak:

"Now that He has stood, He will not sit again until the last battle is over. He has been seated until the time when His enemies are to be put under His feet. The time has now come. The legions of angels that have been standing ready since the night of His passion have now been released upon the earth. The hordes of hell have also been released.

"This is the time for which all of creation has been waiting," he continued. "The great mystery of God will soon be finished. We will now fight until the end. We will fight alongside you and your brethren."

PART V

the overcomers

As I continued walking away from the judgment seat, I began to reflect on all that I had just experienced. It had been both terrible and wonderful. As challenging and heart-rending as it had been, I felt more secure than I ever had. At first it had not been easy to be stripped so bare in front of so many, unable to hide even a single thought. But when I just relaxed and accepted it, knowing that it was cleansing my very soul, it became profoundly liberating. Having nothing to hide was like casting off the heaviest yoke and the strongest shackles. I began to feel as if I could breathe like I had never breathed before.

The more at ease I became, the more my mind seemed to increase in its capacity. Then I began to sense a communication going on which no human words could articulate. I thought of the apostle Paul's comments about his visit to the third heaven, where he had heard inexpressible words. There is a spiritual communication that greatly transcends any form of human communication. It is more profound and meaningful than human words are able to articulate. Somehow it is a pure communication of the heart and mind together, so pure that there is no possibility of misunderstanding.

As I looked at someone in the room, I began to understand what he was thinking, just as he had been able to understand me. When I looked at the Lord, I began to understand Him in the same way. We continued to use words, but the meaning of each one had a depth that no dictionary could have ever captured. My mind had been freed so that its capacity was multiplied many times over. It was exhilarating beyond any previous experience.

The Spirit's Communication

It was also obvious that the Lord was enjoying being able to communicate this way with me as much as I was with Him. Never before had I understood so deeply what it meant for Him to be the Word of God. Jesus is the Communication of God to His creation. His words are spirit and life, and their meaning and power greatly exceed our present human definitions.

Human words are a very superficial form of the communication of the spirit. God created us with the ability to communicate on a level that far transcends human words, but because of the fall and the debacle at the Tower of Babel, we lost this capacity. We cannot be who we were created to be until we regain this, and we can only attain it when we are freed in His presence.

I began to understand that when Adam's transgression caused him to hide from God, it was the beginning of a most terrible distortion of what man was created to be. It brought about a severe reduction of our intellectual and spiritual capacities. These can only be restored when we "come out of hiding" and are genuinely transparent. This means opening ourselves to God and to each other. It is as we behold the glory of the Lord with an "unveiled face" that we are changed into His image. The veils, caused by our hiding, must be discarded.

The Lord's first question to Adam after his transgression was, "Where are you?" In the same way, it is the first question that we must answer if we are to be fully restored to Him. Of course, the Lord knew where Adam was. The question was for Adam's sake. That question was the beginning of God's quest for man.

The story of redemption is God's pursuit of man, not man's pursuit of God. When we can fully answer this question, knowing where we are in relation to God, we will have been fully restored to Him. But we can only know the answer to this question when we are in His presence.

That was the essence of my entire experience at the judgment seat. The Lord already knew all there was to know about me. The whole experience was for my sake, so I would know where I was. It was all to bring me out of hiding, to bring me out of darkness and into the light.

I also began to understand just how much the Lord desired to be one with His people. Through the entire judgment, He was not trying to get me to see something as good or bad as much as to see it in union with Him. The Lord was seeking me more than I was seeking Him. His judgments set me free, and His judgment of the world will set the world free.

The darkness in the world has been perpetuated by our compulsion to hide, which began immediately after the fall. "Walking in the light" is more than just knowing and obeying certain truths—it is *being* true and being free from the compulsion to hide. When judgment day comes, it will bring the final deliverance of Adam from his hiding place. Not only will it be the final liberation of Adam, but it will also begin the final liberation of the creation, which was subject to bondage because of Adam.

"Walking in the light" means no more hiding—from God or anyone else. The nakedness of Adam and Eve before the fall was not just physical, but spiritual as well. When our salvation is complete, we will know this kind of transparency again. To be completely open to others will unlock realms we do not presently even know exist. This is what Satan is attempting to counterfeit through the New Age Movement.

Wisdom Returns

As I walked, pondering all that I had learned, the Lord suddenly appeared by my side again in the form of Wisdom. He now appeared far more glorious than I had ever seen Him, even when He was on the judgment seat. I was both stunned and overjoyed.

"Lord, are you returning with me like this?" I asked.

"I will always be with you like this. However, I want to be even more to you than the way you see Me now. You have seen My kindness and My severity here, but you still do not fully know Me as the Righteous Judge."

This surprised me. I had just spent a considerable amount of time before His judgment seat, and felt that all I had been learning pertained to His judgment. He paused to let this sink in, and then continued:

"There is a freedom that comes when you perceive truth, but whomever I set free is free indeed. The freedom of My presence is greater than just knowing truth. You have experienced liberation in My presence, but there is yet much more for you to understand about

My judgments. When I judge, I am not seeking to condemn or to justify, but to bring forth righteousness. Righteousness is only found in union with Me. That is the righteous judgment—bringing men into unity with Me.

"My church is now clothed with shame because she does not have judges. She does not have judges because she does not know Me as the Judge. I will now raise up judges for My people who know My judgment. They will not only decide between people or issues; they will make things right, which means bringing them into agreement with Me.

"When I appeared to Joshua as the Captain of the Host, I declared that I was neither for him nor his enemies. I never come to take sides. When I come, it is to take over—not to take sides. I appeared as the Captain of the Host before Israel could enter her Promised Land. The church is now about to enter her Promised Land, and I am again about to appear as the Captain of the Host. When I do, I will remove all who have been forcing My people to take sides against their brothers.

"My justice does not take sides in human conflicts, even those involving My people. What I was doing through Israel, I was doing for their enemies, too—not against them. It is only because you see from the earthly, temporal perspective that you do not see My justice. You must see My justice in order to walk in My authority, because righteousness and justice are the foundation of My throne.

"I have imputed righteousness to the people I have chosen. But like Israel in the wilderness, even the greatest saints of the church age have only aligned themselves with My ways a small portion of the time, or with a small part of their minds and hearts. I am not for them or against their enemies, but I am coming to use My people to save their enemies. I love all men and desire for all to be saved."

Brethren Used by the Enemy

I could not help thinking about the great battle we had fought on the mountain. We had wounded many of our own brethren as we fought against the evil controlling them. Many of them were still in the camp of the enemy, either being used by him or kept as his prisoners. I started to wonder if the next battle would be against our own brothers again. The Lord was watching me ponder all of this, and then He continued:

"Until the last battle is over, there will always be some of our brothers who are being used by the enemy. But that is not why I am telling you this now. I am telling you this to help you see how the enemy gets into your own heart and mind, and how he uses you! Even now, you still do not see everything the way that I do.

"This is common with My people. At this time, even My greatest leaders are seldom in harmony with Me. Many are doing good works, but very few are doing what I have called them to do. This is largely the result of divisions among you. I am not coming

to take sides with any one group, but I am calling for those who will come over to My side.

"You are impressed when I give you a 'word of knowledge' about someone's physical illness, or some other knowledge that is not known to you. This knowledge comes when you touch My mind to just a small degree. I know all things. If you were to fully have My mind you would be able to know everything about everyone you encounter, just as you have begun to experience here. You would see all men just the way that I see them. But even then, there is more to fully abiding in Me. To know how to use such knowledge rightly, you must have My heart. Only then will you have My judgment.

"I can only trust you with My supernatural knowledge to the degree that you know My heart. The gifts of the Spirit that I have released to My church are but small tokens of the powers of the age to come. I have called you to be messengers of that age, and you must therefore know its powers. You should earnestly desire the gifts because they are a part of Me, and I have given them to you so that you can be like Me. You are right to seek to know My mind, My ways and My purposes, but you must also earnestly desire to know My heart. When you know My heart, then the eyes of your heart will be opened. Then you will see as I see, and you will do what I do.

"I am about to entrust much more of the powers of the age to come to My church. However, there is a great deception that often comes upon those who are trusted with great power. If you do not understand what I am about to show you, you too will fall to this deception.

"You have asked for My grace, and you shall have it. The first grace that will keep you on the path of life is to know the level of your present deception. Deception involves anything that you do not understand as I do. Knowing the level of your present deception brings humility, and I give My grace to the humble.

"That is why I said, 'Who is so blind but My servant . . .' And that is why I told the Pharisees, 'It is for judgment that I came into the world . . . to give sight to those who do not see, and to make blind those who see . . . If you were blind you would not be guilty, but because you claim to see, your guilt remains.' That is also why My light struck Paul blind when I called him. My light only revealed his true condition. Like him, you must be struck blind in the natural so that you can see by My Spirit."

The Apostle's Advice

I then felt compelled to look at those who were sitting on the thrones we were passing. As I did, my gaze fell upon a man I knew was the apostle Paul. As I looked back at the Lord, He motioned for me to speak to him.

"I have so looked forward to this," I said, feeling awkward but excited by this meeting. "I know that you are aware of how much your letters have guided the church, and they are probably still accomplishing more than all the rest of us put together. You are still one of the greatest lights on earth."

163

"Thank you," he said graciously. "But you do not understand just how much we have looked forward to meeting all of you. You are soldiers in the last battle; you are the ones everyone here is waiting to meet. We only saw these days dimly through our limited prophetic vision, but you have been chosen to live in them. You are soldiers preparing for the last battle. You are the ones we have all been waiting for."

Still feeling awkward, I continued, "But there is no way that I can convey the appreciation we feel for you and for the others who helped set our course with their lives and their writings. I also know we will have an eternity for exchanging our appreciation, so please, while I am here, let me ask, 'What would you say to my generation that will help us in this battle?'"

"I can only say to you now what I have already said to you through my writings," Paul stated, looking me resolutely in the eyes. "However, you will understand them better if you realize that I fell short of all that I was called to do."

"But you are here, on one of the greatest thrones!" I protested. "You are still reaping more fruit for eternal life than any of us could ever hope to reap."

"By the grace of God I was able to finish my course, but I still did not walk in all that I was called to. I fell short of the highest purposes I could have walked in—everyone has. I know that some would practically consider it blasphemy to think of me as anything less than the greatest example of Christian ministry, yet I was being honest when I wrote near the end of my life that I was the greatest of sinners. I was not saying that I *had been* the greatest of sinners, but rather that I was the greatest of sinners *then*. Even though I had been given so much understanding, I walked in comparatively little of it."

"How could that possibly be?" I asked. "I thought you were just being humble."

"True humility is agreement with the truth. Do not fear. My letters were true, and they were written by the anointing of the Holy Spirit. However, I was given so much, and I did not use all that I was given. I, too, fell short. Everyone here has fallen short, except One. The reason you must see this particularly about me is that many are still distorting my teachings, because they have a distorted view of me."

"As you saw the progression in my letters, I went from feeling that I was not inferior to even the most eminent apostles, to acknowledging that I was the least of the apostles. I then saw that I was the least of the saints, and finally that I was the greatest of sinners. I was not just being humble, but I was speaking sober truth. I was entrusted with much more than I used. There is only One here who fully believed, who fully obeyed, and who truly finished all that He was given to do. But you can walk in much more than I did."

Rediscovering the Foundation

Rather feebly, I replied, "I know that what you are saying is true, but are you sure this is the most important message you could give to us for the last battle?"

"I am sure!" he replied with utter conviction. "I so appreciate the grace of the Lord to use my letters as He has, but I am concerned with the way many of you are using them improperly. They are the truth of the Holy Spirit and they are Scripture. The Lord did give me great stones to set into the structure of His eternal church, but they are not foundation stones. The foundation stones were laid by Jesus alone. My life and ministry are not the example of what you are called to be; Jesus alone is that.

"If what I have written is used as a foundation, it will not be able to hold the weight of that which needs to be built upon it. What I have written must be built upon the only Foundation that can withstand what you are about to endure; it must not be used as the foundation. You must see my teachings through the Lord's teachings, not try to understand Him from my perspective. His words are the foundation. I have only built upon them by elaborating on His words. The greatest wisdom and the most powerful truths are His words, not mine.

"It is important for you to know that I did not walk in all that was available to me. There is much more available for every believer to walk in than I did. All true believers have the Holy Spirit in them. The power of the One who created all things lives within them. The least of the saints has the power to move mountains, to stop armies, or to raise the dead.

"If you are to accomplish all that you are called to do in your day, my ministry must not be viewed as the ultimate but merely as a starting place. Your goal must not be to be like me, but to be like the Lord. You can be like Him and do everything that He did, and even more, because He saved His best wine for last."

I reminded myself that only truth could be spoken here. I knew that Paul was right concerning the wrong use of his teachings as a foundation, rather than building upon the foundation of the Gospels. But it was still hard for me to accept that Paul had fallen short of his calling.

I looked at Paul's throne and the glory of his being. It was much more than I ever dreamed the greatest saints in heaven would have. He was every bit as forthright and resolute as I had expected him to be. It struck me how obvious it was that he still carried his great concern for all of the churches. I had idolized him, and that was a transgression he was trying to set me free from. Even so, he was much greater than the Paul I had idolized. Knowing what I was thinking, he put both hands on my shoulders and looked me in the eyes even more resolutely.

"I am your brother. I love you, as everyone here does. But you must understand that our course is now finished. We can neither add to nor take away from what we planted on the earth, but you can. We are not your hope. You are now *our* hope. Even in this conversation I can only confirm what I have already written, but you still have much writing to do. Worship only God, and grow up in all things into Him. Never make any man your goal, but only Him.

"Many will soon walk the earth who will do much greater works than we did. The first shall be last, and the last, first. We do not mind this. It is the joy of our hearts, because we are one with you. The Lord used my generation to lay and begin building upon the foundation, and we will always have the honor of participating in that. But every floor built upon the foundation should go higher. We will not be the building we are supposed to be unless you go higher."

The Ministry and the Message

As I pondered this, he watched me closely. Then he continued, "There are two things we attained in our time that were lost very quickly by the church. They have not yet been recovered, but you must recover them."

"What are they?" I inquired, feeling that what he was about to say was more than just an addendum to what he had already shared with me.

"You must recover the *ministry* and the *message*," he said emphatically.

I looked at the Lord, and He nodded His affirmation, adding, *"It is right that Paul should say this to you. Until this time he has been the most faithful with both of these."*

"Please explain," I implored Paul.

"All right," he replied. "Except for a few places in the world where there are great persecutions or difficulties, we can hardly recognize either the ministry or the message that is being preached today. Therefore, the church is now but a phantom of what it was even in our time, and we were far from all we were called to be. When we served, being in ministry was the greatest sacrifice that one could make, and this reflected the message of the greatest sacrifice that was made—the cross.

"The cross is the power of God, and it is the center of all we are called to live by. You now have so little power to transform the minds and hearts of the believers because you do not live, and do not preach, the cross. Therefore, we have difficulty seeing much difference between the church and the heathen. That is not the gospel or the salvation with which we were entrusted. You must return to the cross."

With those words, he squeezed my shoulders like a father, and then returned to his seat. I felt as if I had received both an incredible blessing and a profound rebuke. As I walked away, I began thinking about the level of Salvation on the mountain, and the treasures of salvation I had seen inside the mountain. I began to see that most of my own decisions—even the decision to enter the door that led me here—were based mainly on what would get me further, not on a consideration of the will of the Lord.

I was still living for myself, not for Him. Even in my desire to embrace the judgments here, I was motivated by what would help me make it back in victory without suffering loss. I was still walking much more in self-centeredness than in Christ-centeredness.

The Last-Day Church

I knew the short talk with Paul would have consequences that would take a long time to fully understand. In a way, I felt that I had received a blessing from the entire eternal church. We really were being cheered on by the great cloud of witnesses. They looked at us like proud parents who wanted better things for their children than they themselves had known. Their greatest joy would be to see the church in the last days become everything the church in their day had failed to attain. I also knew I was still falling far short of what they had prepared for us to walk in.

170

"The last-day church will not be greater than Paul's generation, even if she does greater works," the Lord interjected. *"All that is done is done by My grace. However, I will make more of My grace and power available to the last-day church, because she must accomplish more than the church in any age has yet accomplished.*

"Last-day believers will walk in all the power that I demonstrated, and more, because they will be the final representatives of all who have gone before them. The church will demonstrate My nature and My ways as they have never been demonstrated before by men. It is because I am giving you more grace, and to whom much is given much will be required."

This just made me think even more about Paul. "How could we even become as dedicated and faithful as he had been?" I thought to myself.

"I am not asking you to attain that," the Lord answered. *"I am asking you to abide in Me. You cannot continue to measure yourself by others—not even Paul. You will always fall short of the one you look to, but if you are looking to Me you will go far beyond what you would have otherwise accomplished. As you yourself have taught, it was when the two on the road to Emmaus saw Me break the bread that their eyes were opened. When you read Paul's letters, or anyone else's writings, you must hear Me. Only when you receive your bread directly from Me will the eyes of your heart be opened.*

"You can be distracted the most by those who are the most like Me if you do not see through them to see Me. There is also another

*trap for those who come to know more of My anointing and power
than others. They are often distracted by looking at themselves. As I
was saying before you talked to Paul, My servants must become blind
so that they can see. I let you talk to him then because he is one of
My best examples of this. It was because of My grace that I allowed
him to persecute My church. When he saw My light, he understood
that his own reasoning had led him into direct conflict with the very
truth he claimed to be serving.*

*"Your reasoning will always do that. It will lead you to do
that which is exactly contrary to My will. Greater anointing brings
greater danger of this happening to you, if you do not learn what
Paul did. If you do not take up your cross every day, laying down
all that you are and all that you have before it, you will fall because
of the authority and power that I will give you. Until you learn to
do all things for the sake of the gospel, the more influence that you
have, the greater the danger of this you will face.*

*"Sometimes My anointed ones are deceived into thinking that
because I give them a little supernatural knowledge or power, their
ways must therefore be My ways, and everything they think must be
what I think. This is a great deception, and many have stumbled
because of it. You think like Me when you are in perfect union with
Me. Even with the most anointed who have yet walked the
earth—such as Paul—this union has only been partial, and for brief
periods of time.*

"Paul walked with Me as close as any man ever has. Even so, he was also beset by fears and weaknesses that were not from Me. I could have delivered him from these, as he requested several times, but I had a reason for not delivering him. Paul's great wisdom was to embrace his weaknesses, understanding that if I had delivered him from them, I would not have been able to trust him with the level of revelation and power that I did.

"Paul recognized his own weaknesses and learned to distinguish between them and the revelation of My Spirit. When he was beset with weakness or fear, he knew he was not seeing from My perspective, but from his own. This caused him to seek Me and depend on Me even more. He was also careful not to confuse what came from his own mind and heart with the thoughts of My mind and heart. Therefore I could trust him with revelations that I could not entrust to others."

The Quest

I began to think about how clear all of this was here, but how very often, even after I have had a great experience like this, I still forget it so easily. It is easy to understand and to walk in the light here, but back in the battle it becomes cloudy again. I also thought about how I was not so much beset with fears—as Paul was—but my tendencies were impatience and anger, which were just as much a distortion of the perspective we should have by abiding in the Holy Spirit.

Wisdom stopped and turned to me. *"You are an earthen vessel, and that is all you will be while you walk the earth. However, you can see Me just as clearly there as you do here, if you will look with the eyes of your heart. You can be just as close to Me there as anyone has ever been to Me, and even more so.*

"I have made the way for everyone to be as close to Me as they truly desire to be. If you really desire to be even closer to Me than Paul was, you can. Some will want this, and they will want it badly enough to give themselves fully to it, laying aside anything that hinders their intimacy with Me. They will have what they seek.

"If it is your quest to walk on earth just as you can walk with Me here, I will be just as close to you there as I am now. If you seek Me, you will find Me. If you draw near to Me, I will draw near to you. It is My desire to set a table for you right in the midst of your enemies. This is not just My desire for My leaders, but for all who call upon My name. I want to be much closer to you, and to everyone who calls upon Me, than I have yet been able to be with anyone who has lived on earth. You determine how close we will be, not I. I will be found by those who seek Me.

"You are here because you asked for My judgment in your life. You sought Me as the Judge and now you are finding Me. But you must not think that just because you have seen My judgment seat, now all of your judgments will be My judgments. You will only have My judgments as you walk in unity with Me and seek the anointing of My Spirit. This can be gained or lost every day.

"I have let you see angels and given you many dreams and visions, because you kept asking for them. I love to give My children the good gifts that they ask for. For years you asked Me for wisdom, so you are receiving it. You have asked Me to judge you, so you are receiving my judgment. But these experiences do not make you fully wise, nor do they make you a righteous judge. You will only have wisdom and judgment as you abide in Me.

"Do not ever stop seeking Me. The more you mature, the more you will know your desperate need for Me. The more you mature, the less you will seek to hide—from Me or others—for your desire will be to always walk in the light.

"You have seen Me as Savior, Lord, Wisdom and Judge. When you return to the battle, you can still see My judgment seat with the eyes of your heart. When you walk in the knowledge that all you think and do are fully revealed here, you will have the freedom to live there just as you do here. It is only when you hide, from Me or others, that the veils return to hide Me from you. I am Truth, and those who worship Me must do so in Spirit and Truth.

"Truth is never found hiding in the darkness, but always seeks to remain in the light. Light exposes and makes manifest. Only when you seek to be exposed, and allow who you are in your heart to be exposed, will you walk in the light as I am in the light. True fellowship with Me requires complete exposure. True fellowship with My people requires the same.

175

"When you stood before the judgment seat, you felt more freedom and security than you have ever felt, because you did not have to hide anymore. You felt more security because you knew that My judgments were true and righteous. The moral and spiritual order of My universe is just as sure as the natural order established upon the natural laws. You trust My law of gravity without even thinking about it. You must learn to trust My judgments in the same way. My standards of righteousness are unchanging, and are just as sure. To live by this truth is to walk in faith. True faith is to have confidence in who I am.

The Power of His Word

"You seek to know and walk in My power so that you can heal the sick and perform miracles, but you have not even begun to comprehend the power of My word. To resurrect all the dead who have ever lived on earth will not even cause Me to strain. I uphold all things by the power of My word. The creation exists because of My word, and it is held together by My word.

"Before the end, I will reveal My power on earth. Even so, the greatest power that I have ever revealed on the earth, or ever will, is still a very small demonstration of My power. I do not reveal My power to cause men to believe in My power, but to cause men to believe in My love.

"If I had wanted to save the world with My power when I walked the earth, I could have moved mountains by pointing a finger. Then all men would have bowed to Me, but not because they

loved Me or loved the truth, but because they feared My power. I do not want men to obey Me because they fear My power, but because they love Me and love the truth.

"If you do not know My love, then My power will corrupt you. I do not give you love so you can know My power, but I give you power so that you can know My love. The goal of your life must be love, not power. Then I will give you power with which to love people. I will give you the power to heal the sick because you love them, and I love them, and I do not want them sick.

"So you must seek love first, and then faith. You cannot please Me without faith. But faith is not just the knowledge of My power, it is the knowledge of My love and the power of My love. Faith must first be exercised in order to receive more love. Seek faith to love more, and to do more with your love. Only when you seek the faith to love can I trust you with My power. Faith works by love.

"My word is the power that upholds all things. To the degree that you believe My word is true, you can do all things. Those who really believe that My words are true, will also be true to their own words. It is My nature to be true, and the creation trusts My word because I am faithful to it.

"Those who are like Me are also true to their own words. Their word is sure, and their commitments are trustworthy. Their 'yes' means 'yes,' and their 'no' means 'no.' If your own words are not true, you will also begin to doubt My words, because deception is in your heart. If you are not faithful to your own *words, it is because you do not really know Me. To have faith, you must be faithful. I have called you to walk by faith because I am faithful. It is My nature.*

"That is why you will be judged because of the careless words you speak. To be careless is to care less. Words have power, and those who are careless with words cannot be trusted with the power of My word. It is wisdom to be careful with your words, and to keep them as I do Mine."

The Lord's words were rolling over me like great waves from the sea. I felt like Job before the whirlwind. I thought that I was getting smaller and smaller, and then realized that He was getting larger. I had never felt so presumptuous. How could I have been so casual with God? I felt like an ant staring up at a mountain range. I was less than dust, yet He was taking the time to speak to me. I could not stand any more, and turned away.

After a few moments, I felt a reassuring hand on my shoulder. It was Wisdom. His glory was even greater now, but He was again my size. *"Do you understand what happened just then?"* He asked.

Knowing very well that when the Lord asks a question He is not seeking information, I began to ponder what had happened. I knew that it was reality. Compared to Him, I am less than a speck of dust would be to the earth, and for some reason He wanted me to experience that realization in a profound way.

Answering my thoughts, He elaborated:

"What you are thinking is true, but this comparison of man to God is not just in size. You began to experience the power of My words. To be entrusted with My words is to be entrusted with the power by which the universe is held together. I did not do this to make you feel small, but to help you understand the seriousness and the power of that with which you have been entrusted—the word of God.

"In all of your endeavors, remember that the importance of a single word from God to man is of more value than all of the treasures on earth. You must understand and teach My brethren to respect the value of My word. As one who is called to carry My words, you must also respect the value of your own words. Those who will carry the truth must be true."

Meeting the Evangelist

While hearing these words, I felt compelled to look up toward one of the thrones beside me. Immediately I saw a man I recognized. He had been a great evangelist when I was a child, and many felt that he had walked in more power than anyone since the early church. I had read about him and had listened to some of his recorded messages. It was hard not to be touched by his genuine humility, and the obvious love he had for the Lord and people. Even so, I also felt that some of his teachings had gone seriously awry. I was surprised, but also relieved, to see him sitting on a great throne. I was captured by the humility and love that still exuded from him.

As I turned to ask the Lord if I could talk with this man, I could see how much the Lord loved him. However, the Lord motioned for me to continue walking, and would not permit me to speak with the evangelist.

"I just wanted you to see him here," the Lord explained, *"and to understand the position that he has with Me. There is much for you to understand about him. He was a messenger to My last-day church, but the church could not hear him for reasons that you will understand in due time. He did fall into discouragement and delusion for a time, and his message was distorted. It must be recovered, as well as the parts that I have given to others which were also distorted."*

Knowing that everything here happened in perfect timing with all that I was meant to learn, I began to think about how seeing this man must be related to what we had just talked about—the potential of power to corrupt.

"Yes. There is a great danger in walking in great power," the Lord responded. *"It has happened to many of My messengers, and that is part of the message they are to give to My last-day church. You must walk in My power, and even much greater power than*

these experienced. But if you ever start to think that the power is My endorsement of you, or even of your message, you will open the door to the same delusion. The Holy Spirit is given to testify only of Me. If you are wise, like Paul, you will learn to glory more in your weaknesses than in your strengths.

"True faith is the true recognition of who I am. It is nothing more and nothing less. But you must always remember—even if you abide in My presence and see Me as I am—you can still fall if you turn from Me to look back at yourself. That is how Lucifer fell. He dwelt in this room and beheld My glory and the glory of My Father. However, he began to look at himself more than he looked to us. He then began to take pride in his position and power.

Many of My servants who have been allowed to see My glory and be entrusted with My power have fallen in the same way as Lucifer. If you begin to think that it is because of your wisdom, your righteousness, or even your devotion to pure doctrine, you will stumble too."

Confidence

I knew that this was as severe a warning as anything that I had been told here. I wanted to go back and fight in the last battle, but I was having serious questions about being able to do so without falling into the traps that now seemed to be everywhere. I looked back at the Lord. He was Wisdom, and I thought of how badly I needed to know Him as Wisdom when I returned.

"It is good for you to lose confidence in yourself. I cannot trust you with the powers of the age to come until you do. The more confidence you lose in yourself, the more power I will be able to trust you with, if . . ."

I waited a long time for the Lord to continue, but He didn't. Somehow I knew that He wanted me to continue the sentence, but I did not know what to say. However, the more I looked at Him, the more confidence I felt. Finally I knew what to say.

"If I put my confidence in you," I added.

"Yes. You must have faith to do what you are called to do, but it must be faith in Me. It is not enough for you to just lose confidence in yourself. That only leads to insecurity if you do not fill the void with confidence in Me. That is how many of these men fell to their delusions.

"Many of these men and women were prophets. But some of them, out of insecurity, would not let men call them prophets. Yet that was not the truth, because they were. False humility is also a deception. If the enemy could deceive them into thinking that they were not really prophets, he could also deceive them into thinking that they were greater prophets than they were, just by nurturing their self-confidence. False humility will not cast out pride. It is just another form of self-centeredness, which the enemy has a right to exploit.

"All of your failures will be the result of this one thing: self-centeredness. The only way to be delivered from this is to walk in love. Love does not seek its own."

As I was thinking about all of this, a wonderful clarity began to come. I could see the whole experience from beginning to end, having as its focus a single, simple message. "How easily I am beguiled from the simplicity of devotion to You," I lamented.

The Smile of the Lord

The Lord then stopped and looked at me with an expression I pray that I will never forget. He smiled. I did not want to abuse this opportunity, but I somehow felt that when He smiled like that I could ask Him anything and He would give it to me. So I took the chance.

"Lord, when you said, 'Let there be light,' there was light. You prayed in John 17 that we would love you with the same love that the Father loved you with. Will you please say to me now, 'Let there be love in you,' so that I will love you with the Father's love?"

He did not quit smiling, but rather put His arm around me like a friend. *"I already said that to you, before the creation of the world when I called you. I have also said it to your brethren who will fight along with you in the last battle. You will know My Father's love for Me. It is a perfect love that will cast out all of your fears.*

This love will enable you to believe Me so you can do the works that I did, and even greater works, because I am with My Father. You will know His love for Me, and the works you will be given to do will glorify Me. Now, for your sake, I say again, 'Let there be My Father's love in you.'"

I was overwhelmed with appreciation for this whole experience. "I love your judgments," I said. I then started to turn and look back at the judgment seat, but the Lord stopped me.

"Don't look back. I am not there for you now; I am here. I will lead you from this room and back to your place in the battle, but you must not look back. You must see My judgment seat in your own heart, because that is where it is now."

"Just like the Garden, and like the treasures of salvation . . ." I thought to myself.

"Yes. Everything that I am doing, I am doing in your heart. That is where the living waters flow. That is where I am."

He then gestured toward me, so I looked at myself, pulling back the cloak of humility. I was stunned by what I saw. My armor contained the same glory that surrounded Him. I quickly covered it again with my cloak.

"I also prayed to My Father on the night before My crucifixion that the glory I had with Him in the beginning would be with My people, so that you will be one. It is My glory that unifies. As you

come together with others who love Me, My glory will be magnified. The more My glory is magnified by the joining of those who love Me, the more the world will know that I was sent by the Father. Now the world really will know that you are My disciples because you will love Me, and you will love each other."

As I kept looking at Him, my confidence continued to grow. It was like being washed on the inside. Soon I was feeling ready to do anything He asked.

Angelo

"There is still someone you must meet before you return to the battle," He said as we walked. As we did, I continued to be astonished by how much more glorious He had become than even a few minutes before.

"Every time you see Me with the eyes of your heart, your mind is renewed a little bit more," He proceeded to say. *"One day you will be able to abide in My presence continually. When you do that, all you have learned by My Spirit will be readily available to you, and I will be available to you."*

I could hear and understand everything He said, but I was so captured by His glory that I just had to ask Him, "Lord, why are you so much more glorious now than when You first appeared to me as Wisdom?"

"I have never changed, but you have. You are changed as you behold My glory with an unveiled face. The experiences you have

had are removing the veils from your face so that you can see Me more clearly. Yet nothing removes them as quickly as when you behold My love."

He then stopped, and I turned to look at those on the thrones next to us. We were still in the place where the highest kings were sitting. Then I recognized a man who was close by.

"Sir, I know you from somewhere, but I simply cannot remember where."

"You once saw me in a vision," he replied.

I immediately remembered, and was shocked! "So you were a real person?"

"Yes," he replied.

I remembered the day when, as a young Christian, I had become frustrated with some issues in my life. I went out into the middle of a battlefield park near my apartment and determined that I would wait until the Lord spoke to me. As I sat reading my Bible, I was caught up into a vision, one of the first ones I ever had.

In the vision I saw a man who was zealously serving the Lord. He was continually witnessing to people, teaching the Bible, and visiting the sick to pray for them. He was very zealous for the Lord, and had a genuine love for people. Then I saw another man, named Angelo, who was obviously a tramp or a homeless person. When a small kitten wandered into his path, he started to kick it but restrained himself, though he still shoved it out of the way rather harshly with his foot. Then the Lord asked me which of these men pleased Him the most.

"The first," I said without hesitating.

"No, the second," He responded, and began to tell me their stories.

He shared that the first man had been raised in a wonderful family, which had always known the Lord. He grew up in a thriving church and then attended one of the best Bible colleges in the country. He had been given one hundred portions of His love, but he was using only seventy-five.

The second man had been born deaf. He was abused and kept in a dark, cold attic until he was found by the authorities when he was eight years old. He had then been shifted from one institution to another, where the abuse continued. Finally, he was turned out on the streets. The Lord had only given him three portions of His love to help him overcome all of this, but he had mustered every bit of it to fight the rage in his heart and keep from hurting the kitten.

I now looked at that man, a king sitting on a throne far more glorious than Solomon could have even imagined. Hosts of angels were arrayed about him, waiting to do his bidding. I turned to the Lord in awe. I still could not believe he was real, much less one of the great kings.

"Lord, please tell me the rest of His story," I begged.

"Of course, that is why we are here. Angelo was so faithful with the little I had given to him that I gave him three more portions of My love. He used all of that to quit stealing. He almost starved, but he refused to take anything that was not his. He bought his food with what he could make collecting bottles, and occasionally he found someone who would let him do yard work.

"Angelo could not hear, but he had learned to read, so I sent him a gospel tract. As he read it, the Spirit opened his heart, and he gave his life to Me. I again doubled the portions of My love to Him, and he faithfully used all of them. He wanted to share Me with others, but he could not speak. Even though he lived in such poverty, he started spending over half of everything he made on gospel tracts to give out on street corners."

"How many did he lead to you?" I asked, thinking that it must have been multitudes for him to be sitting with the kings.

"One," the Lord answered. *"In order to encourage him, I let him lead a dying alcoholic to Me. It encouraged him so much that he would have stood on that corner for many more years just to bring another soul to repentance. But all of heaven was entreating Me to bring him here quickly, and I, too, wanted him to receive his reward."*

A Different Kind of Martyr

"But what did Angelo do to become a king here?" I asked.

"He was faithful with all that he was given. He overcame all until he became like Me, and he died a martyr."

"But what did he overcome, and how was he martyred?"

"He overcame the world with My love. Very few have overcome so much with so little. Many of My people dwell in homes with conveniences that kings would have envied just a century ago, yet they do not appreciate them. Angelo, on the other hand, would so appreciate even a cardboard box on a cold night that he would turn it into a glorious temple of My presence.

"Angelo began to love everyone and everything. He would rejoice more over an apple than some of My people do over a great feast. He was faithful with all that I gave him, even though it was not very much compared to what I gave others, including you. I showed him to you in a vision because you passed by him many times. Once you even pointed him out to one of your friends and spoke of him."

"I did? What did I say?"

"You said, 'There is another one of those Elijahs who must have escaped from the bus station.' You said he was 'a religious nut' who was sent by the enemy to turn people off to the gospel."

This was the worst blow I had yet suffered in this whole experience. I was more than shocked, I was appalled. I tried to remember the specific incident, but couldn't—simply because there were so many others like it. I had never had much compassion for filthy street preachers, considering them tools of Satan sent to turn people off to the gospel.

"I'm sorry, Lord. I'm really sorry."

"You are forgiven," He quickly responded. *"And you are right that there are many who try to preach the gospel on the streets for wrong or even perverted reasons. Even so, there are many who are sincere, even if they are untrained and unlearned. You must not judge by appearances. There are as many true servants who look like he did as there are among the polished professionals in the great cathedrals and organizations that men have built in My Name."*

He then motioned for me to look up at Angelo. When I had turned, he had descended the steps to his throne and was now right in front of me. Opening his arms, he gave me a great hug and kissed my forehead like a father. Love poured over me and through me until I felt that it would overload my nervous system. When he finally released me, I was staggering as if I were drunk, but it was a wonderful feeling. It was love like I had never felt before.

"He could have imparted that to you on earth," the Lord continued. *"He had much to give to My people, but they would not come near him. Even My prophets avoided him. He grew in the faith by buying a Bible and a couple of books that he read over and over. He tried to go to churches, but he could not find one that would*

receive him. *If they would have taken him in, they would have taken Me in. He was My knock upon their door.*"

I was learning a new definition of grief. "How did he die?" I asked, remembering that he had been martyred. Based on what I had seen so far, I was half expecting that I somehow was even responsible for that.

"*He froze to death trying to keep alive an old wino who had passed out in the cold.*"

The Unlikely Overcomer

As I looked at Angelo, I could not believe how hard my heart had been. Even so, I did not understand how dying in this way made him a martyr, which I thought was a title reserved for those who died because they would not compromise their testimony of the lordship of Christ.

"Lord, I know that he is truly an overcomer," I remarked. "And it truly is warranted for him to be here. But are those who die in such a way actually considered martyrs?"

"*Angelo was a martyr every day that he lived. He would only do enough for himself to stay alive, and he gladly sacrificed his life to save a needy friend. As Paul wrote to the Corinthians, even if you give your body to be burned, but do not have love, it counts as nothing. But, when you give yourself with love, it counts for much.*

191

"Angelo died every day, because he did not live for himself, but for others. Even though he always considered himself the least of the saints, he was truly one of the greatest. As you have already learned, many of those who consider themselves the greatest, and are considered by others to be the greatest, end up being the least here. Angelo did not die for a doctrine, or even for his testimony, but he did die for Me."

"Lord, please help me to remember this. When I return, please do not let me forget what I am seeing here," I begged.

"That is why I am with you here, and I will be with you when you return. Wisdom is to see with My eyes, and to not judge by appearances. I showed you Angelo in the vision so that you would recognize him when you passed him on the street. If you had shared with him the knowledge of his past that I had shown you in the vision, he would have given his life to me then. You could have then discipled this great king, and he would have had a great impact on My church.

"If My people would look at others the way I do, Angelo and many others like him would have been recognized. They would have been paraded into the greatest pulpits. My people would have come from the ends of the earth to sit at their feet, because by doing this they would have sat at My feet. He would have taught you to love, and how to invest the gifts that I have given you so that you could bear much more fruit."

I was so ashamed that I did not want to even look at the Lord, but finally I turned back to Him as I felt the pain driving me toward self-centeredness again. When I looked at Him, I was virtually blinded by His glory. It took a while, but gradually my eyes adjusted so that I could see Him.

"Remember that you are forgiven," He said. *"I am not showing you these things to condemn you, but to teach you. Always remember that compassion will remove the veils from your soul faster than anything else."*

As we began to walk again, Angelo entreated me, "Please remember my friends, the homeless. Many will love our Savior if someone will go to them."

His words had such power in them that I was too moved to answer, so I just nodded. I knew that those words were the decree of a great king, and a great friend of the King of Kings.

"Lord, will you help me to help the homeless?" I asked.

"I will help any who help them," He responded. *"When you love those whom I love, you will always know My help. They will be given the Helper by the measure of their love. You have asked many times for more of My anointing; that is how you will receive it. Love those whom I love. As you love them, you love Me. As you give to them, you have given to Me, and I will give more to you in return."*

193

Living Like a King

My mind drifted to my nice home and all the other possessions I had. I was not wealthy, yet I knew that by earthly standards I lived much better than kings had just a century before. I had never felt guilty about it before, but I did now. Somehow it was a good feeling, but at the same time it did not feel right. Again I looked back to the Lord, for I knew He would help me.

"Remember what I said about how My perfect law of love made light and darkness distinct. When confusion such as you are now feeling comes, you know that what you are experiencing is not My perfect law of love. I delight in giving My family good gifts, just as you do yours. I want you to enjoy them and appreciate them. Nevertheless, you must not worship them, and you must freely share them when I call you to.

"I could wave My hand and instantly remove all poverty from the earth. There will be a day of reckoning when the mountains and high places are brought down, and the poor and oppressed are raised up, but I must do it. Human compassion is just as contrary to Me as human oppression. Human compassion is used as a substitute for the power of My cross. I have not called you to sacrifice, but to obey. Sometimes you will have to sacrifice in order to obey Me, but if your sacrifice is not done in obedience, it will separate us.

"You are guilty for the way you misjudged and treated this great king when he was My servant on earth. Do not judge anyone

without inquiring of Me. You have missed more of the encounters I have set up for you than you have ever imagined, simply because you were not sensitive to Me. However, I did not show you this to just make you feel guilty, but rather to bring you to repentance so you will not continue to miss such opportunities.

"If you just react in guilt, you will begin to do things to compensate for your guilt, which is an affront to My cross. My cross alone can remove your guilt. And because I went to the cross to remove your guilt, whatever is done in guilt is not done for Me.

"I do not enjoy seeing men suffer," Wisdom continued. *"But human compassion will not lead them to the cross, which alone can relieve their real suffering. You missed Angelo because you were not walking in compassion. You will have more when you return, but your compassion must still be subject to My Spirit. Even I did not heal all those for whom I had compassion, but I only did what I saw My Father doing. You must not just do things out of compassion, but in obedience to My Spirit. Only then will your compassion have the power of redemption.*

"I have given you the gifts of My Spirit. You have known My anointing in your preaching and writing, but you have known it much less than you realize. Rarely do you really see with My eyes or hear with My ears or understand with My heart. Without Me, you can do nothing that will benefit My kingdom or promote My gospel.

"You have fought in My battles, and you have even seen the top of My mountain. You have learned to shoot arrows of truth and

hit the enemy. You have learned a little about using My sword. But remember, love is My greatest weapon. Love will never fail. Love will be the power that destroys the works of the devil. And love will be what brings My kingdom. Love is the banner over My army, and under this banner you must now fight."

With this, we turned into a corridor and were no longer in the great hall of judgment. The glory of Wisdom was all around me, but I could no longer see Him distinctly. Suddenly, I came to a door. My first impulse was to turn because I did not want to leave, but I knew that I must. This was the door Wisdom had led me to. I had to go through it.

To be continued . . .

epilogue

This book stems from an extraordinary dream the Lord gave me in early 1995, which was the first of a number of related prophetic experiences. I published a condensed version of the first dream in *The Morning Star Prophetic Bulletin* and *The Morning Star Journal* under the title **"The Hordes of Hell Are Marching."** As I continued to seek the Lord about this great spiritual battle I had seen, I received a series of related visions and prophetic experiences. Condensed versions of these were published in *The Morning Star Journal* as **"The Hordes of Hell Are Marching, Parts II & III."**

The articles in this series became probably the most popular writings we have ever published. We were deluged with requests to have all three parts published together in a book. I determined to do this, and set out to fill in all that had been left out of the condensed versions. However, just when I was ready to give this to our editing department, I had another prophetic experience that was obviously related to this vision, containing what I felt were the most important parts of all. These are included in **Parts IV & V** of this book (some of **Part IV** was published in **Part III** in *The Journal*). A considerable amount of previously unpublished material is also included in the first three parts of this book.

How I Received the Vision

One of the most common questions I receive about this vision concerns how I received it. That is an important question, and I will attempt to briefly answer it here. First, I must explain what I mean by visions and "prophetic experiences."

Prophetic experiences, as I call them, are numerous and diverse. They include all the primary ways God spoke to His people in the Scriptures. Because the Lord is the same today as He was yesterday, He has never ceased to speak to His people in similar ways. The same supernatural experiences found in the Scriptures can be seen throughout church history.

In his sermon on the day of Pentecost, the apostle Peter explained that dreams, visions and prophecy are primary signs of the outpouring of the Holy Spirit in the last days (see Acts 2:14-22). As we are obviously getting closer to the end of this age, these signs are becoming increasingly common.

One reason why experiences such as dreams, visions and prophecy are becoming so much more common now is because we will need them for accomplishing our purposes in these times. It is also true that Satan, who unfortunately knows the Scriptures better than many Christians, understands the importance of prophetic revelation in God's relationship with His people. Satan is therefore pouring out his own counterfeit gifts in great measure to those who serve him. However, there would be no counterfeit if there were not a genuine reality, just as there are no counterfeit three-dollar bills because there are no real ones.

Soon after I became a Christian in 1972, I read Peter's sermon in Acts chapter two and understood that if we were in the end times, it was important to understand these ways the Lord would be speaking to us. I do not remember praying at first to have the experiences myself, but I did begin having them, which gave me an even greater impetus for understanding them.

Since that time, I have gone through periods when prophetic experiences were very frequent. I have also gone through long periods of time when I did not have such experiences. Yet, after each period of not having them, they returned, and were either much more powerful or much more frequent. Lately they have been both. Through all of this I have learned a great deal about prophetic gifts and prophetic people, and I am planning to address the full scope of the prophetic ministry in a book soon to be released.

Different Levels of Revelation

There are many levels of prophetic revelation. The beginning levels include prophetic "impressions." These are genuine revelations. They can be extraordinarily specific and accurate when interpreted by those who are experienced and sensitive to them. However, on this level our "revelations" can be affected by our own feelings, prejudices and doctrines. I have therefore resolved not to use such expressions as "thus saith the Lord" with any revelations that come on this level.

Visions can also come on the impression level. They are gentle, and must be seen with "the eyes of our heart." These, too, can be very specific and accurate, especially when received and/or interpreted by those who are experienced. The more the "eyes of our hearts" are opened, as Paul prayed in Ephesians 1:18, the more powerful and useful these can be.

The next level of revelation is a conscious sense of the presence of the Lord, or the anointing of the Holy Spirit, which gives special illumination to our minds. This often comes when I am writing or speaking, and it gives me much greater confidence in the importance or accuracy of what I am saying. However, while we may be emboldened by this sense of God's presence, we need to realize that this is still a level where we can be influenced by our preexisting viewpoints and attitudes. I believe this is why, in certain matters, Paul would say he was giving his *opinion*, but that he *thought* he had [the agreement of] the Spirit of the Lord (see I Corinthians 7:40). In general, we need humility rather than dogmatism when we deal with the prophetic.

"Open visions" occur on a higher level than impressions, and they tend to give us even more clarity than we have when we feel the presence of the Lord or the anointing. Open visions are external, and are viewed with the clarity of a movie screen. Since they cannot be controlled by us, there is far less possibility of mixture in revelations that come this way.

Another higher-level prophetic experience is a trance, which is like dreaming when you are awake. Instead of just seeing a "screen" like in an open vision, you feel as if you are *in* the movie—actually *there* in some strange way. Peter fell into a trance in Acts 10:10, when he was instructed to go to the house of Cornelius and preach the gospel to the Gentiles for the first time. Paul, likewise, refers in Acts 22:17 to a trance he experienced while praying in the temple.

Trances were common experiences of the biblical prophets. The depth of trances can range from being rather mild—so that you are still conscious of your physical surroundings and can even still interact with them—to feeling as if you are literally in the place of your vision. This seems to be what Ezekiel experienced rather frequently, and what John probably experienced when he had the visions recorded in the book of Revelation.

The visions contained in this book all began with dreams. Some of them came under a very intense sense of the presence of the Lord, but the overwhelming majority were received in some level of a trance. Usually the visions came on a level where I was still conscious of my surroundings, and could even interact with them, such as answering the phone. When they were interrupted, or when things got so intense I would have to get up and walk around, the vision would immediately continue once I sat down again. One time the experience became so intense that I actually got up and left the mountain cabin where I go to seek the Lord, and drove home. Over a week later, I returned and almost immediately was right back where I left off.

I have never known how to "turn on" such experiences, but I have almost always had the liberty to turn them off at will. Twice, large portions of this vision came at what I considered to be very inconvenient times, when I had gone to my cabin to get some important work done while facing deadlines. Two of our issues of *The Morning Star Journal* were a little late going out because of this, and one of my books was delayed a few months from when I had hoped to finish it. However, the Lord does not seem to be very concerned about our deadlines!

In the dream and the trances, I had what I consider to be greatly magnified gifts of discernment and words of knowledge. Sometimes when I look at a person or pray for a church or ministry, I just start to know things about them of which I have no natural knowledge. During the prophetic experiences recorded in this book, these gifts were operating on a level that I have never personally experienced in "real life." For example, in this vision I could look at a division of the evil horde and immediately know all of its strategies and capabilities.

I do not know how this enhanced knowledge came to me, but I just knew it, and in great detail. At times I would look at things or people and know their past, present and future all at once. To save time and space in this book, I have included this knowledge just as matter of fact, without going into an explanation of how I received it.

Using Prophetic Revelations

I must state emphatically that I do not believe that any kind of prophetic revelation is for the purpose of establishing doctrine. We have the Scriptures for that. There are two basic uses for the prophetic. The first is for revealing the present or future strategic will of the Lord in certain matters. We have examples of this in Paul's dream to go to Macedonia

(Acts 16:6-10) and in the trance where he was told to quickly leave Jerusalem (Acts 22:17-18). We also have examples of this in the ministry of Agabus. One of these concerned a famine that was coming upon the whole world (Acts 11:27-30), and the other had to do with Paul's visit to Jerusalem (Acts 21:10-12).

Such revelations are also given for illuminating doctrine that is taught in the Scripture, but is not clearly understood. For example, Peter's trance in Acts 10 not only illuminated God's will for Peter; it also provided timely insight on a matter the Scriptures were very clear about (the Gentiles being able to receive the gospel), but which had not yet been understood by the church.

While the visions in this book do contain some strategic revelations, they also shed light on some biblical doctrines that I honestly had not seen before, but now see quite clearly. However, for years I had known and taught most of the truths illuminated to me in these experiences, even though I cannot say that I had lived them all very well. Many times I thought about the warning Paul gave Timothy to pay attention to his own teachings (I Timothy 4:16). Confronted by my failure to live up to some of my own teachings, I therefore accepted many of these messages as a personal rebuke. Even so, I also felt they were general messages to the body of Christ, and so I included them here.

Some of my friends encouraged me to write this as an allegory, in the third person like *The Pilgrim's Progress*. I decided against that for several reasons. First, I feel that some would have taken this to be the result of my own creativity, which would have been wrong. I would like to be this creative, but I am not.

Another reason was that I felt I could be much more accurate if I related these experiences just as I received them, and I endeavored to do so. However, I consider my memory of details to be one of my greatest weaknesses. At times I have questioned my memory of certain details in this vision, and you should therefore have the liberty to question some of the details too. I think such scrutiny is wise with any such messages. Only the Scriptures deserve to be considered infallible. As you consider these experiences I had, I pray that the Holy Spirit will lead you to the truth and separate any chaff that may be present from the wheat.

Rick Joyner

the call

Rick Joyner

MorningStar
PUBLICATIONS

The Call

by Rick Joyner

International Standard Book Number 1-878327-84-4.

Unless otherwise stated, all Scripture quotations are taken from the New American Standard Bible, copyright © 1960, 1962, 1963, 1968, 1971, 1973, 1974, 1977, by The Lockman Foundation.

Italics in Scripture references are for emphasis only.

Cover art and design by Dianne C. Thomas.

This book is dedicated to the Ministry
Team and Staff at MorningStar
Publications and Ministries. Your
devotion to excellence, integrity and
sacrificial service for the sake of the
gospel is a great inspiration to me and
is bearing fruit that will never perish.

CONTENTS

introduction

This is the second book in *The Final Quest* Series. Although *The Call* begins where the first book ends, it is possible to read this one and generally understand its message without having read the first book. However, if you have not yet read *The Final Quest*, some of the material may seem disconnected. Since this is a continuing spiritual saga, there are some foundations laid in the first book that are built upon in the second.

As I explained in the introduction to *The Final Quest*, these books are the result of a series of "prophetic experiences." Many times I have been advised that they would be received by more people if I had written them as fictional allegory. That may be true, but it is not my goal to have these books read by more people, but to simply remain faithful to the messages with which I have been entrusted, conveying them as accurately as I can. For me to claim that these are the result of my own creativity would be both dishonest and an affront to the Spirit of Truth.

Even so, because *The Final Quest* has been widely received across the spectrum of Christian denominations and movements and has found remarkable favor with conservative evangelicals, I want to explain in more depth what I mean by "prophetic experiences," how I received these in particular, and a little about the biblical basis for these experiences in our own times.

Biblical prophetic experiences are very diverse in nature, as were those which I received in this unfolding series. Some came in dreams, others in visions, and still others in what the Bible calls "trances." Dreams, visions and trances all have biblical precedents and are established ways that the Lord speaks to His people. There is such an increasing number of Christians who are having such experiences today that it is regarded by some to be a fulfillment of Peter's prophecy on the Day of Pentecost which he quoted from the prophet Joel:

"And it shall be in the last days," God says, "That I will pour forth of My Spirit upon all mankind; and your sons and your daughters shall prophesy, and your young men shall see visions, and your old men shall dream dreams;

Even upon My bondslaves, both men and women, I will in those days pour forth of My Spirit and they shall prophesy" (Acts 2:17-18).

As this Scripture declares, prophetic revelations through visions, dreams and prophecies will be prevalent in the last days. Because there is such a dramatic increase in revelation being given to Christians in these times, it is understandable why it is regarded as a sign that we are indeed in the "last days."

Discerning the True From the False

Jesus also warned that in the last days there would be many **"false prophets" (Matthew 24:24)**. This is to be expected because as the Lord also taught, whenever He sows wheat in a field, the enemy comes along and sows tares in the same field (Matthew 13:24-30). Tares look like wheat, and may even taste like wheat, but they are noxious. Satan will immediately try to counterfeit everything that God is doing, creating confusion and, if possible, deceiving even the elect. However, Satan could not do this if God did not allow it. Obviously the Lord wants us to learn to distinguish the real from the false and allow the real to be tested by the false in order to purify that which is true.

That false prophets are also becoming more prevalent should not surprise us, but rather encourage us to seek the real with greater determination. If we do not want to be deceived by the false, the answer is not to reject all prophecy, but rather to know what is true. Those who cannot discern true prophecy in the times to come will be increasingly subject to the false. If God is planting something, it is because we will need it. If we do not plant a field, but rather neglect it, the only harvest reaped will be weeds. Those who do not receive what God is doing today will end up reaping that which grows wild.

From the beginning, the Lord was committed to allowing mankind to choose between the real and the false, the good and the evil. That is why He put the Tree of the Knowledge of Good and Evil in the Garden along with the Tree of Life. He did not put the Tree of Knowledge there in order to cause us to stumble, but rather so that we could prove our obedience and love for Him. There can be no true obedience from the heart unless there is the freedom to disobey.

Likewise, true teachers and true teaching will always be shadowed by false teachers and false teaching; true prophets and true prophecy will always be shadowed by the false. The Lord allows the enemy to sow tares among the wheat in order to test our hearts. Those who love the truth will discern what is true, and those who are pure in heart will discern that which is pure.

That the Lord would warn us that there will be false prophets at the end of the age implies that there will be true ones, or He simply would have said that at the end of the age, all prophets will be false. Some do believe that all prophets at the end will be false, but this is a basic conflict with Joel's prophecy that at the end, God will pour out His Spirit and there will be visions, dreams and prophecy (Joel 2:28-29).

There is a danger in being open to prophetic revelations such as dreams, visions, and prophecy. However, there is a much greater danger if we are not open to them. Revelations are not given to us for our entertainment, but because we need them for the times in which we live. As Jesus also declared,

> **"Truly, truly, I say to you, he who does not enter by the door into the fold of the sheep, but climbs up some other way, he is a thief and a robber.**
>
> **"But he who enters by the door is a shepherd of the sheep.**
>
> **"To him the doorkeeper opens, and the sheep hear his voice, and he calls his own sheep by name, and leads them out.**
>
> **"When he puts forth all his own, he goes before them, and the sheep follow him because they know his voice.**
>
> **"And a stranger they simply will not follow, but will flee from him, because they do not know the voice of strangers" (John 10:1-5).**

The Lord's sheep know His voice. They are not deceived by strangers because they know His voice so well they can distinguish it from the voices of others. One of the ways that the Lord has spoken to His people from earliest times has been prophetically. Because we know that God never changes, and because the Scriptures are so clear about the visions, dreams, and prophecies that He will give to His people, it is imperative for us to distinguish His revelation from the enemy's and then to interpret His messages correctly. After they are interpreted correctly, we must then have the wisdom to apply them correctly.

The Purpose of Prophecy

Prophecy is given for encouragement, but it is also given for edification. To edify means "to build." Much of my life and ministry has been built on fulfilled prophetic words. Almost every major aspect of our ministry, including the places where I go to minister or speak, is foretold prophetically. I do not consider doing something or going somewhere to minister unless the Lord has spoken to me in advance. Jesus did the same. He did not respond to human needs: He only did what He saw the Father doing. We do not have time to go places or start things that God is not leading us to do. I think that our devotion to hearing from the Lord before we do things enables us to be fruitful with the resources and time entrusted to us.

I know of others who have successfully built a ministry or church on prophetic words. I also know of some who have been shipwrecked and others who suffered serious diversions because they did not know how to judge prophecy. Many of these problems happened because they received genuine revelation from the Lord, but misinterpreted or misapplied

16

it. For some, this may sound too complicated, but it is the process clearly established by the Scriptures, and we will pay a dear price if we deviate from sound biblical wisdom in regard to prophetic revelation.

As Jesus said in Matthew 22:29, **"Ye do err not knowing the Scriptures or the power of God"** (KJV). Many today make errors because they know the Scriptures but do not know the power of God. Those who know His power often make mistakes because they do not know the Scriptures as they should. If we are going to keep from making mistakes, we must know both the Scriptures *and* the power of God. Prophecy was never intended to replace the Bible, and the Bible was never intended to replace prophecy.

I have spent many hours with conservative evangelical leaders of major ministries to whom God has begun speaking through dreams, visions and prophecy. In many cases, He began to do this even when it violated their theology. This has become so widespread that I have begun to wonder if there are any conservative evangelical leaders with whom God is not dealing in this way. At MorningStar, there is almost a steady stream of contacts from those who are seeking help in understanding what is happening to them. What they may not understand at this point is that prophetic people also need their help every bit as much as conservative evangelicals need the help of those who have some experience with the prophetic gifts. For the church to achieve the maturity to which she is called, there must be a union between those who know the Scriptures and those who know the power of God, and this is now happening at a fast pace.

I have searched the Bible to verify that the teachings given in my experiences are biblical, and I am confident that they are. I do admit that some of them caused me to view certain Scriptures in a way that I had not previously seen them. Even so, I believe that this is consistent with the purpose of such prophetic revelations. *Prophecy should not be used to establish doctrine.* We were given the Bible for that, and I believe that the doctrine of the Bible is complete and must never be added to. However, the Bible itself has many examples of prophetic experiences given to individuals for the purpose of illuminating the Scriptures.

A prominent New Testament example of this would be the trance into which Peter fell, resulting in his trip to Cornelius' house and opening the door of faith to the Gentiles. This experience and the fruit it bore clarified for the church that the Lord also intended for the gospel to be preached to the Gentiles. This did not establish a new doctrine, but illuminated what the Scriptures said and what the Lord, Himself, had taught when He was with them, but which they apparently had forgotten.

Many of the experiences included in these two books did the same for me. They constantly reminded me of my own teachings and teachings I had heard from others, but at best had only superficially implemented in my life. In this way, these prophetic experiences were a constant challenge to me, bringing essential correction, and even judgment, to my own life and teachings. As I was the one having the experiences, I took them personally and do not presume that the same corrections are needed by everyone. However, I do believe that many of them, if not most of them, are generally applicable to the church in our time.

There are a number of recurring themes in this discourse. Not only are there repetitious statements, but some of these themes are repeated from different perspectives or worded differently in various situations. I realize that this may have been done because of my own dullness, just as it seemed that the Lord had to repeat himself over and over to Peter. I also realize that such repetition is not good literary style, but style is not my goal here. Each time something is repeated, the probability that it will be retained is increased. I have therefore tried to repeat everything just as it was repeated to me.

Prophetic Experiences

I also understand how the nature of some of these revelations would cause theological problems for some. One of these would certainly be the way that I met and talked with many Old and New Testament characters, as well as prominent people in church history who are now dead. There are biblical precedents for this, such as when the Lord talked to Moses and Elijah. Even though Elijah was carried up without dying, Moses had died. We also have the example when the apostle John fell down to worship the angel in Revelation 22:9. The angel rebuked John, declaring that he, too, was a fellow servant of his brethren (Revelation 22:9). Many have understood this to indicate that this was one of the saints who had gone on to be with the Lord.

Even so, I can understand how some would still have a problem with this, and there is another explanation. There is a difference between prophetic experiences and actually doing something. For example, when Ezekiel was caught up in the Spirit and carried to Jerusalem, it is obvious that he was not taken to the actual Jerusalem, even though it seemed very real to him. Much of what he experienced did not actually exist, but was meant to convey a message to the exiles.

Likewise, even though some of these experiences and people seemed very real to me, I seriously question whether I was actually talking to people in heaven. I believe that these were prophetic experiences meant to convey a message. I do not know if the places I saw in heaven were actual places or appeared to me in the way that they did for the purpose of conveying that message. However, I am open to the thought that I saw real places and met real people. I see no conflict with Scripture that would prohibit this possibility, although I understand how some would object. Even so, just as Abel still speaks though he is dead, certainly the lives of biblical characters are messages, and these experiences helped to illuminate this to me more than ever before.

One reason that I lean toward the belief that these were prophetic experiences and that I was not talking with the real people is because of how long they did or did not last. For example, most people have had dreams that were so real that when they awoke, for a brief time they may actually believe that the dreams were real. However, even the most realistic of dreams usually begins to fade so that in just a couple of hours, it can be forgotten. Real experiences are not that way. I have had real encounters with the Lord and with angels that are almost as real to me now as they were years ago when I first experienced them. I have had many dreams and visions in which I saw the Lord or angels, but these would quickly fade. Except for a very few of my experiences included in these books, these prophetic episodes faded like revelations rather than enduring like real encounters.

It was for this reason that I tried to write down these experiences as quickly as I could after having them. In some cases, I was not able to do this. When I was able to get to a place where I could write them down, my memory of them had already begun to fade. I did feel the Holy Spirit helping to bring things to my remembrance, but the more time that elapsed between the experience and the time in which I was able to record them, the more concerned I was that they may have not been conveyed exactly as I received them.

In such cases, I was aware that my own pet doctrines or prejudices could easily creep into my writing, and though I sincerely tried not to let this happen, I acknowledge the possibility that this could have occurred in some instances. For this reason, my continual prayer for this book has been for the Holy Spirit to lead me in writing it and also to lead everyone who reads it. He was given to lead us to the truth and to Jesus. My prayer is that you will discern that which is truth and that which is from Jesus, holding fast to that which is and discarding anything that isn't.

Infallibility of Scripture

Though there are many places where I tried to write the exact words of the Lord as they were spoken to me, this is not Scripture, and I do not believe that any prophetic experience is intended to carry the weight of Scripture. Even so, prophecy is very important for the church or we would not have been exhorted by the Scripture to **"Pursue love, yet desire earnestly spiritual gifts, but especially that you may *prophesy"* (I Corinthians 14:1).** We are told that **"But one who prophesies speaks to men for edification and exhortation and consolation. One who speaks in a tongue edifies himself; but one who prophesies edifies the church" (I Corinthians 14:3-4).** Never are we told that prophecy is for the purpose of teaching doctrine—we have the Scriptures for that. Never are we told that prophecy is infallible, which is why we must judge prophecy. However, prophecy does edify.

Because prophecy is a gift of the Holy Spirit, we must treat everything that comes from Him as holy, but because it comes through humans, it must not be considered infallible.

The Scriptures, as they were originally written, are infallible. They are the rock of truth and pure revelation of God and His ways upon which we can build our lives with the surety that Scripture will stand forever. I view prophecy more like the manna that the Lord served in the wilderness. It is from the Lord and will help to sustain us in our day-by-day walks, but if we try to keep it longer than intended, it will become foul.

The Scriptures are permanent and given so that we can build our lives upon truth, while prophecy is given for edification and encouragement, strategically keeping us in the day-to-day will of the Lord. The quality of any relationship will be determined by the quality of the communication, and any relationship that does not have continuing communication is a dying relationship. Prophecy does help to keep our day-to-day relationship with the Lord fresh, which is why I believe that the Scripture encourages us to **"especially"** seek this gift.

I have sought the gift of prophecy for many years. I did this out of obedience to the Scripture that exhorts us to do this because I love the prophetic gifts. I love prophetic experiences, even though all but a few have been major rebukes for me. Even so, I have prayed much more often for wisdom and the gift of a word of wisdom than I have for any of the other gifts. That is why I think that the Lord almost always appears to me in these experiences personified as Wisdom. I also think that a truly wise person loves rebukes, because **"reproofs for discipline are the way of life" (Proverbs 6:23).** In every one of these experiences, I received a profound and badly needed correction in my life.

In this book, there are also some very basic corrections for the church in general. Except for the churches for which I have personal responsibility, I try not to see the problems that are afflicting the body of Christ. The church is the Lord's bride, and I am very cautious about any way that I would presume to bring correction to her. Just as Paul explained to the Corinthians, we have spheres of authority within which we must stay.

It is not right for me to correct someone else's children, but as a friend, I may speak to the parents and hope that they also would feel the liberty to speak to me if they see things which need correcting in my children. However, in the experiences included in this book, the Lord showed me that the church today is headed for some terrible catastrophes if we do not make some very basic course corrections. I consider myself as having these problems, too, and therefore if you ask me what we should do about them, all I can say now is that I also am trying to work them out. I am seeking more revelation, a greater understanding in the interpretation, and the wisdom to apply all this correctly.

I encourage you again to keep in mind that even though the prophetic experiences I had when I received these messages were very real when they took place, they would often seem unreal to me only hours later. That was sometimes a problem when I tried to record these experiences. I did my best to write them as faithfully as I could, but I by no means claim that these are the exact words spoken to me or that everything written about these experiences is written exactly as they occurred. However, even though I may have forgotten some of the details or did not always get the wording right, the message is true, it is from the Lord, and the time is near.

Rick Joyner
November 1998

CHAPTER I

the glory

I stood looking at the door that I was to enter next. It was plain and uninviting. As I turned to view once again the Great Hall of Judgment, I was overwhelmed by its glory and expanse. I did not want to leave here even though the evil of my own heart was continually exposed. Although the process was painful, it was so liberating that I did not want it to stop. I actually yearned for more conviction.

"And you shall have more," Wisdom interjected, knowing my thoughts. *"What you have found here will go with you. However, you do not have to come here to be changed. The power of the cross is enough to change you. What you have experienced here you can experience every day. The Holy Spirit was sent to convict you of sin, to lead you to truth, and to testify of Me. He is with you continually. You must get to know the Holy Spirit better.*

"Many believe in the Holy Spirit, but few make room for Him in their lives. As the end of this age approaches that will change.

29

The Holy Spirit is about to move over the earth as He did in the beginning. He will take the chaos and confusion that are spreading across the earth, and He will bring forth the glorious new creation right in the midst of it. You are about to enter the times when He will do wonders continually, and the whole world will be in awe of His works.

"He will do all of this through My people. When the Holy Spirit moves, the sons and daughters of God will prophesy. From the old to the young they will dream dreams and see visions. The works that I did, and greater works, will they do in My name, that I might be glorified in the earth. The whole creation groans and travails for what the Holy Spirit is about to do.

"What you will find through that door will help you to prepare for what is to come. I am the Savior, but I am also the Judge. I am about to reveal Myself to the world as the Righteous Judge. First, I must reveal My judgment to My own household. My people are about to know the fellowship of the Holy Spirit. Then they will know His power to convict of sin. They will also know that He will always lead them to the truth that will set them free. This is the truth that testifies of Me. When My people have come to know Me as I AM, then I will use them to testify of Me.

"I am the Judge, but it is better for you to judge yourself so that I will not have to judge you. Even so, My judgments are about to be restored to My people. I will judge My own household first. After that I will judge the whole earth."

The glory of Wisdom was overshadowing everything around me. I had never seen such splendor before, even here. It increased as He talked about His judgments. I knew by this that there was a glory to be seen by knowing Him as the Judge that was greater than I had known before. I started feeling so small and insignificant in His presence that it was hard for me to concentrate on what He was saying. Just when I thought I would be overwhelmed by His glory, He reached out and touched me on the forehead, gently but firmly. When He did this, my mind became focused and clear.

"You began to look at yourself. This will always bring confusion, making it harder for you to hear Me. Every time you experience My touch, your mind will become clearer. Every time you feel My presence, know that I have come to touch you in order that you may see Me and hear Me. You must learn to abide in My presence without becoming self-conscious and self-absorbed. This causes you to turn from the truth that is in Me and turn to the deception that is in your fallen nature.

"Many people fall when My Spirit touches them. The time for falling is over. You must learn to stand when My Spirit moves. If you do not stand when My Spirit moves, He cannot use you. The heathen should fall before Me, but I need for My people to stand so that I can use them."

The Pride of False Humility

I heard irritation in the Lord's voice when He said this. I felt that it was like the irritation He seemed to have with His disciples in the gospels. Immediately I understood that His irritation usually came when they started looking at their inadequacies or failures.

"Lord, I'm sorry," I pleaded, "but your presence is so overwhelming. How do I keep from feeling so small when I'm close to you like this?"

"You are small, but you must learn to abide in My presence without looking at yourself. You will not be able to hear from Me or speak for Me if you are looking at yourself. You will always be inadequate. You will always be unworthy for what I call you to do, but it will never be your adequacy or worthiness that causes Me to use you. You must not look at your inadequacy, but look to My adequacy. You must stop looking at your own unworthiness and look to My righteousness. When you are used, it is because of who I am, not who you are.

"You did feel My anger as you began to look at yourself. This is the anger I felt toward Moses when he started to complain about how inadequate he was. This only reveals that you are looking to yourself more than to Me, which is the main reason why I am able to use so few of My people for what I desire to do. This false humility is actually a form of the pride that caused the fall of man. Adam and Eve began to feel inadequate and that they needed to be more

32

than I had made them to be. They took it upon themselves to make themselves into who they should be. You can never make yourself into who you should be, but you must trust Me to make you into who you should be."

Although I had never related false humility to the fall of man in the Garden, I knew that this was a major stumbling block preventing many from becoming useful to the Lord, and I had taught on this many times. Now in His presence, my own false humility was revealed in me and looked even worse than I had ever seen it in anyone else. This form of pride was repulsive, and I could understand why it caused the anger of the Lord to burn.

In His presence, all that we are is soon revealed, and even after all of the judgment I had just endured, I still had some of the most basic flaws that kept me from knowing Him and serving Him as I was called to do. As shocking as this was, I did not want to dwell on myself any longer, so I turned to look at Him, desiring to see as much of His glory as I could endure while He was with me in this way. Immediately, my gloom turned into ecstasy. My knees wanted to buckle, but I was determined to stand for as long as I could.

Soon after, I awoke. For days afterward, I felt an energy surging through me making everything look glorious. I loved everything that I saw. A doorknob seemed wonderful beyond comprehension. Old houses and cars were so beautiful to me that I was sorry I was not an artist so that I could capture their beauty and nobility. Trees and animals all seemed like very special personal friends. Every person I saw was like a library of revelation and meaning, and I was so thankful for eternity so that I could get to know them all. I could not look at anything without seeing magnificence, hardly believing that I had walked through so much of my life and missed so much.

Yet, for all of this wonderful emotion and revelation I felt flowing through me, I did not know what to do with it. I knew that if I did not learn how to use it for good that it would fade, which it did in just a few days. It was as if the meaning of life was slipping from me, and I knew that I had to recover it. What I had experienced was more wonderful than any drug, and I was addicted. This was the result of seeing His glory, and I had to see more. I desired to learn how to *abide* in His presence and to allow His life to flow through me in order to touch others. I had to abide in the Holy Spirit and allow Him to use me. *This was my call.*

CHAPTER II

two witnesses

For days I had been in a deep depression. Everything seemed so bleak. Even the very sound of people irritated me, and any disruption to what I wanted to do angered me. I thought the worst of everyone and had to fight to contain the black thoughts that arose in me toward them. I felt as if I had slipped into hell and was sliding deeper into it each day. I finally cried out to the Lord and almost immediately found myself standing in front of the door with Wisdom standing next to me.

"Lord, I am sorry. I slipped from Your presence all the way into hell it seems."

"The whole world still lies in the power of the evil one," He replied, *"and you walk on the edge of hell every day. Through the midst of it, there is a path of life. There are deep ditches on either side of the path of life, so you must not deviate from the narrow way."*

"Well, I fell into one of the ditches and could not find my way out."

"No one can find their own way out of those ditches. Following your own way is how you fall into them, and your own way will never lead you out. I am the only way out. When you fall, do not waste your time trying to figure everything out, for you will only sink deeper into the mire. Just ask for help. I am your Shepherd, and I will always help you when you call on Me."

"Lord, I don't want to waste time trying to figure everything out, but I would really like to understand how I fell so far, so fast. What caused me to turn from the path of life and fall into the ditch like that? You are Wisdom, and I know that it is wisdom to ask."

"It is wisdom to know when to ask for understanding and when to just ask for help. Here it is wisdom for you to ask. Only when you are in My presence can you understand. Your understanding will always be twisted when you are depressed, and you will never accurately see truth from that place. Depression is the deception that comes from seeing the world from your perspective. Truth comes from seeing the world through My eyes from where I sit, at the right hand of the Father. Like the cherubim in Isaiah 6, those who abide in My presence will say, 'The whole earth is filled with His glory.'"

I remembered how as a new believer, I had read this text and actually thought that these cherubim were deceived. I could not understand how they could say *"The whole earth is filled with His glory,"* when the whole earth seemed to be filled with wars, disease, child abuse, treachery and evil on every side. Then the Lord spoke to me one day and said, *"The reason that these cherubim say that the whole earth is filled with My glory is because they dwell in My presence. When you dwell in My presence, you will not see anything but glory."*

"Lord, I remember you teaching me that, but I have not lived it very well. I have spent much of my life seeing things from the dark side. I guess I have spent much of my life sitting in one of those ditches beside the path of life rather than walking on it."

"That is true," the Lord responded. *"Every now and then you would get up and take a few paces, but then slide off into the ditch on the other side. Even so, you have made some progress, but now it is time for you to stay on the path. You do not have any more time to waste in those ditches."*

The Lord's kindness and patience seemed overwhelming as He continued.

"What caused you to slide into the ditch this last time?" He began.

After thinking about it, I could see that I had become consumed with maintaining the feeling rather than knowing the Source of the feeling.

"I took My eyes off of you," I confessed.

"I know it seems too simple, but this is all that you did, and taking your eyes off of Me is all that you have to do to drift from the path of life. When you abide in Me, you will see nothing but glory. This does not mean that you will not see the conflicts, confusion, darkness and deception that are in the world, but when you see them, you will always see My answer to them. When you abide in Me, you will always see how truth prevails over deception, and you will see the manner in which My kingdom will come."

"Lord, when I am here, this is all more real to me than anything I have experienced on earth, but when I am on earth, all that is here seems like an unreal dream. I know that this is the true reality and that earth is temporary. I also know that if this place were more real to me on earth, I would be able to walk in your wisdom more and stay on the path of life. You have said it is always wisdom to ask. I ask you to make this realm more real to me when I am on the earth. Then I will be able to walk more perfectly in your ways. I also ask you to help me to convey this reality to others. The darkness is growing great on earth, and there are few who have vision. I ask You to give us more of Your power, let us see more of Your glory, and let us know the true judgment that comes from Your presence."

"When you start to live by what you see with the eyes of your heart, you will walk with Me, and you will see My glory. The eyes of your heart are your window into this realm of the Spirit. Through

the eyes of your heart, you may come to My Throne of Grace, at any time. If you will come to Me, I will be more real to you. I will also trust you with more power."

As He spoke, I was compelled to turn and look at the multitudes of kings, princes, friends and servants of the Lord who were all standing in the Hall of Judgment. The wonder and glory of all that occurred there were so great that I would have been satisfied to stay forever. Again I was astounded to think that this place was just the beginning of heaven. But even with all of its wonders, the real wonder of heaven was the presence of the Lord. Here in the beginning of heaven, He was Wisdom and He was the Judge, which are the same.

"Lord," I inquired, "Here you are Wisdom and the Judge, but how are you known in the other realms of heaven?"

"I AM Wisdom and I AM the Judge in every realm, but I AM also much more. Because you have asked, I will show you who I AM. Even so, you have only begun to know Me as Wisdom and Judge. In due time, you will see more of Me, but there is more for you to learn about My judgments first."

The First Witness

"God's judgments are the first step into the heavenly realm," a voice said that I had not heard before. "When the Judgment Day comes, the King will be known to all, and His judgments will be understood. Then the earth will be set free.

You asked for His judgments to come to your own life, now begin asking for them to come to the world."

I turned to see who had spoken. He was of great stature and brilliance, but a little less than the others I had met in the Hall of Judgment. I assumed that he was an angel, but then he said:

"I am Lot. You have been chosen to live in difficult times just as I was chosen. As Abraham lived and interceded for Sodom, you must do the same. During the times when great perversion is released upon the earth, men and women of great faith will also arise. Like Abraham, you must use your faith to intercede for the wicked, and you must also witness the judgment of God coming upon the earth. The Lord cannot abide the increasing evil of mankind much longer. I was silent and many perished. You must not be like me—you must not be silent."

"Tell me more. How do I warn them?" I asked.

"I thought that I would be a warning just by being different. Being different is not enough! The power of the Holy Spirit to convict of sin is released by the spoken word. What the Lord did to Sodom, He did as an example so that others would not have to be destroyed in this way. You can warn those who are headed for destruction by telling them my story. There are now many cities whose evil He will not abide much longer. If those who know the Lord do not arise, there will be many more like Sodom very soon.

"The Judgment Day is coming. All of creation will then know the wisdom of His judgments, but you must not wait for that day. You must seek His judgments every day, and you must make them known on the earth. If His people will walk in His judgments, many on the earth will know of them before the great Day of Judgment. By this many more will be saved. It is His desire that none should be lost, and that none of His people suffer loss on that day.

"The people of the earth are blind. They will not see if you simply try to be a witness. The message of judgment must go forth in *words*. The Holy Spirit anoints words, but the words must be spoken in order for Him to anoint them. "Righteousness and justice are the foundation of His throne. His people have come to know something of His righteousness, but few know His justice. His throne will abide in His house, therefore judgment must begin with His own house.

"You must live by the truth that you have learned here, and you must teach it. His judgments are coming. If His people will walk in His judgment before the Judgment Day, that day will be glorious for them. If they do not live by them, they, too, will know the sorrow that the world is about to know. His judgments would not be true if they were not the same for all. Through you and others, He will entreat His people again to judge themselves lest they be judged. Then you must entreat the world."

Lot directed me to look at the door before which I was standing. It still seemed dark and uninviting, like the doctrines of God's judgment, I thought. The glory of the Lord that surrounded us made it seem even more bleak. Even so, I now knew how glorious His judgment really is. I had also come to understand that almost every door through which He leads us looks bleak at first and then becomes glorious. It almost seems that the bleaker the door looks, the more glorious it will be on the other side. Just passing through His doors takes faith, but they always lead to more glory.

Lot continued with my train of thought. As I had already learned, in this place thoughts are broadcast to all.

"Through that door, you will experience more of His glory. His glory is not just the brilliance that you see around Him or in this place, nor is it merely the feelings that you have while abiding in Him. His glory is also revealed through His judgments. This is not the only way that it is revealed, but it is this way that you were called here to understand. Through that door, you will learn of another way to see His glory. It is by seeing His glory that His people will be changed, and He is about to show them His glory. When they see His glory, they will rejoice in all of His ways, even in His judgments."

The Second Witness

Then a second voice spoke, "I, too, confirm this truth. The judgment of God is about to be revealed on the earth. Even so, 'Mercy triumphs over judgment.' The Lord always extends mercy before judgment. If you will warn the people that His judgments are near, His mercy will save many."

I did not recognize the one speaking, but it was another man of great stature and nobility, with a brilliance that indicated a high rank.

"I am Jonah," he said. "When you understand the Lord's judgments, you understand His ways. However, even if you understand them, it does not mean that you agree with them. Understanding is necessary, but it is not enough. The Lord also wants you to agree with Him.

"You have often asked for the Lord's presence to go with you. That is wisdom. I was a prophet, and I knew Him, yet I tried to flee from His presence. That was a great folly, but not as foolish as you may think. I had come to understand the great burning that comes with His presence. I had come to understand the responsibility that comes from being close to Him. In His presence, all wood, hay and stubble is consumed. When you draw close to Him with hidden sin in your heart, it will drive you to insanity, as many have learned through the ages. I was not trying to flee from the will of the Lord as much as I was fleeing from His presence.

45

"When you ask for the reality of His presence, you are asking for the reality that you have seen here to be with you. Heaven is your true home, and it is right for you to yearn for this. Even so, He is a holy God, and if you will walk closely with Him, you, too, must be holy. The closer that you get to Him, the more deadly hidden sin can be."

"I understand this," I replied. "That is why I asked for the Lord's judgments in my own life."

"Now I must ask you this," Jonah continued. "Will you seek Him? Will you come to Him?"

"Of course," I responded. "I desire His presence more than anything. There is nothing greater than being in His presence. I know that many of my motives for wanting to be with Him are selfish, but being with Him helps to set me free from that kind of selfishness. I do want to be with Him. I will come to Him."

"Will you?" Jonah continued. "Until now you have been even more foolish than I was. You can come boldly before His Throne of Grace at any time and for any need, but rarely do you come. Yearning for His presence is not enough. You must come to Him. If you draw near to Him, He will draw near to you. Why do you not do it? You are always as close to Him as *you* want to be.

"Many have come to know and follow His ways, but they do not come to Him. In the times that you will soon enter, they will depart from His ways because they did not come to Him. You have laughed at my folly, which was great, but yours is even greater than mine. However, I do not laugh at your folly—I weep for you. Your Savior weeps for you; He intercedes for you continually. When He weeps, all of heaven weeps. I weep because I know how foolish His people are. I know you because you are just like me, and like me, the church has run to Tarshish, desiring to trade with the world even more than sitting before His glorious throne. At the same time, the sword of God's judgments are hanging over the earth. I weep for the church because I know you so well."

"I am guilty!" I pleaded. "What can we do?"

"Great storms are coming upon the earth," Jonah continued. "I slept when the storm came upon the ship that I was in while running from the Lord. The church is also sleeping. I was the prophet of God, but the heathen had to wake me up. So it is with the church. The heathen have more discernment than the church at this time. They know when the church is going the wrong way, and they are shaking the church, trying to wake you up so that you will call on your God.

"Soon the leaders of the world will cast you overboard, just as the men in that ship had to do to me. They will not let you keep going in the way you are headed. This is the grace of God to you. He will then discipline you with a great beast that comes up out of the sea. It will swallow you for a time, but you will be vomited out of it. Then you will preach His message."

"Is there no other way?" I asked.

"Yes, there is another way," Jonah replied, "although this has come and is coming. Some are already in the belly of the beast. Some are about to be cast overboard, and some are still sleeping, but almost all have been on the ship going the wrong way, seeking to trade with the world. However, you can judge yourself and He will not have to judge you. If you will wake yourself up, repent and go the way that He sends you, you will not have to be swallowed by the beast."

"Is the beast to which you are referring the one in Revelation 13?" I asked.

"It is the same. As you read in that chapter, this beast is given to make war with the saints and to overcome them. This will happen to all who do not repent. But know that those who are overcome by this first beast will be vomited out of it before the next beast comes, the one that comes up out of the earth. Even so, it will be much easier for you if you repent. It is much better not to be swallowed by the beast.

"Just as Lot's story is a warning to those who are given over to perversion, my story is a warning to the Lord's prophet, the church. The church is running from the presence of the Lord. It is running to activity in place of seeking the Lord's presence. You may call your activity 'ministry,' but it is actually running from the presence of the Lord. As I have said, the church is running to Tarshish so that it can trade with the world and seek the treasures of the sea, while the greater treasures—the treasures of heaven—few are seeking.

"The sin of wanting to trade with the world has entangled the church, just as I was entangled in the belly of the beast with the weeds wrapped around my head. The weeds, the cares of the world, have wrapped themselves around the mind of the church. It took me three days to turn to the Lord because I was so entangled. It is taking Christians much longer. Their minds are so entangled with the world, and they have fallen to such depths, that many have no hope of getting free. You must turn to the Lord instead of away from Him. He can untangle *any* mess, and He can bring you up from the greatest depths. Run *from* Him no longer! Run *to* Him!"

Then Lot added, "Remember the mercy that the Lord had for Nineveh. He had mercy because Jonah preached. He did not live among them and try to be a witness: He preached the Word of God. Power is in the Word. There is no darkness so dark that His Word cannot penetrate it. Many will repent and be saved if you will go to those to whom the Lord sends you and give His warning."

Then Jonah continued, "When you fall short of the Lord's grace and sin entangles you, it is hard for you to come to Him. You must learn to always run to the Lord at such times, not away from Him. When you go through that door, you will enter the times when the Lord's power and glory will be released on the earth such as He has not done since the beginning of time. All of heaven has been waiting for the things that you are about to see. It will also be the time of the greatest darkness. You cannot endure either the glory or the darkness without His grace. You will not walk in His ways without coming to Him daily. You must not only seek His presence, but you must abide in His presence continually.

"Those who have tried to follow Him by just seeking Him once a week in a church service while they spend the rest of the week seeking the world will soon fall away. Those who call upon His name thinking that He is their servant also will soon fall away. He is the Lord of all and all will soon know this! First, His own people must know it, so the judgment is going to begin with His own household.

"It is presumption to only call upon the Lord when you want something. You should call on Him to ask what He wants, not what you want. Many of those who have some faith also have great presumption; the line between the two can be very thin. When God's judgments come to His own household, His people will learn the difference between faith and presumption. Those who try to do His work without Him will fall away. Many have faith in the Lord, but only know

Him from a distance. These do great works in His name, but He does not know them. Those who have known Him from afar will soon weep over their folly.

"God does not exist for the sake of His house—His house exists for Him. In His patience, He has been waiting outside of His own house, knocking, calling, but few have opened to Him. Those who hear the Lord's voice and open to Him will sit with Him at His table. They will also sit with Him on His throne, and they will see the world as He sees it. Presumption cannot sit with Him at His table, nor on His throne. Presumption is the pride that caused the first fall, and all of the darkness and evil that are about to be reaped on the earth have come because of it.

"When Satan saw God's glory, he turned to the way of presumption. Satan dwelt in His presence and still turned from Him. This is the greatest danger for those who see His glory and know His presence. Do not become presumptuous because of what you have seen. Never become proud because of your visions: This will always lead to a fall."

Merciful Judgment

As Jonah spoke, each word was like a hammer blow. I was appalled by my sin. Not only was I ashamed of the way in which I had thought of him, but I was ashamed even more for mocking Jonah for the very same things that I, too, had done.

51

Even though I tried desperately to stand, my knees could not hold me up any longer, and I fell to my face. His words were like being flailed with a whip, but at the same time, the pain was welcome. I knew I needed to hear them, and I did not want Jonah to stop teaching me until all of my evil ways were exposed. The exposing power of the words was great, but it was much more than that. There was a power on them that made any excuse seem appalling. They passed every barrier and went straight to my heart. As I lay on the ground, I felt as though I were undergoing surgery.

Then Lot interjected, "Many believers have made falling down in the Lord's presence frivolous and meaningless, but the church is about to fall under the same power that felled you—conviction. If you fall when you cannot stand then your falling will result in your standing for truth."

Still I did not want to move. I did not want to do anything until I had firmly grasped what Jonah had said. I did not want the conviction to go away until it had done its work. They seemed to understand as there was silence for a time, and then Lot continued.

"Jonah had the greatest preaching anointing yet given to a man. Without miracles or signs, when he preached, one of the most wicked cities that ever existed repented. If Jonah had preached in Sodom, that city would have remained until this day. The power of Jonah's preaching is a sign. When he awakened and was vomited out of the beast, he had this power. This is the power of preaching that will be given to the church in the last days. This is the power of conviction that the Lord is waiting to give His church. When she is vomited out of the beast that has swallowed her, even the most evil will listen to her words. This is the sign of Jonah that will be given to the church. The words of those who experience resurrection from the deep will have power."

I was still stunned. Even so, I was determined to run to the Lord and not away from Him, so I turned to look directly at Wisdom.

"Lord, I, too, can fall away in what is coming! I am guilty of all of these things. I have seen so much of your glory, and still I fall to the traps and diversions that keep me from drawing close to you. Please help me in this. I desperately need Your wisdom, but I also need Your mercy. Please send mercy and help us before You send the judgment that we deserve. I ask for the mercy of the cross."

Wisdom answered, *"You will be given mercy because you have asked for it. I will give you more time. My mercy to you is time. Use this time wisely, for soon there will be no more. The time is near when I can delay no longer. Every day that I delay My judgment is mercy. See it as that and use it wisely.*

"I would always rather show mercy than judgment, but the end is near. The darkness is growing and the time of great trouble will

be upon you soon. If you do not use the time I give you, the coming troubles will overtake you. If you use the time that I give you wisely, you will overcome and prevail. There is one characteristic that is common to the overcomers in every age—they did not waste their time!

"In My mercy, I am giving you this warning. Warn My people that in My mercy, I will no longer let them presume on My mercy. In My mercy, My discipline will be upon them. Warn them not to harden their hearts, but to repent and turn to Me.

"It is true that you, too, can fall away. Your love will grow cold and you will deny Me, if you do not deny yourself and take up your cross every day. Those who seek to save their own life will lose it, but those who lose their life for My sake will find true life. What I will give to My people will be a life of even more abundance than they have asked for, even in their presumption.

"When I have finished judging My own household, I will then send My judgments upon the whole earth. In My righteous judgment, I will show a distinction between My people and those who do not know Me. Now the whole world lies in the power of the evil one. Now he rewards unrighteousness and resists the righteous. When the Judgment Day comes, the whole world will know that I reward righteousness and resist the proud.

"Righteousness and justice are the foundation of My throne. It is because of My justice that I discipline more severely those who know the truth but do not live by it. I have brought you here to see

My judgments. You have gained understanding here, but this will be an even greater judgment to you if you do not walk in what you have seen. To whom much is given, much will be required. Here you have known the mercy of My judgments. If you continue to allow sin to entangle you, you will know the severity of My judgment. Many of My people still love sin. Those who love sin and their own comfort and prosperity more than Me will soon know My severity. These will not stand in the times that are coming.

"I will show severity to the proud and mercy to the humble. The greatest distraction of My people has not been the difficulties, but the prosperity. If My people would seek Me during times of prosperity, I could trust them with even more of the true wealth of My kingdom. I desire for you to have an abundance for every good deed. I want your generosity to overflow. My people will prosper in earthly riches in the times ahead, even in the times of trouble, but the riches will be from Me and not the prince of this present evil age. If I cannot trust you with earthly riches, how can I trust you with the powers of the age to come? You must learn to seek Me as much in prosperity as when you are in poverty. All that I entrust to you is still Mine. I will only entrust more to those who are more obedient.

"Know that the prince of darkness also gives prosperity. He continues to make the same offer to My people that he made to Me. He will give the kingdoms of this world to those who will bow down and worship him and serve him by living according to his ways. There is a prosperity of the world and there is the prosperity of My

kingdom. The coming judgments will help My people to know the difference. The riches of those who have prospered by serving the prince of this evil age and using the ways of this evil age will be a millstone that hangs about their neck when the floods come. All will soon be judged by the truth. Those who prosper by Me do not compromise truth in order to prosper.

"My judgment begins with My household to teach you discipline so that you will walk in obedience. The wages of sin is death, and the wages of righteousness are peace, joy, glory and honor. All are about to receive their worthy wages. This is the judgment, and it is justice that it begins with My own household."

Then Lot and Jonah spoke together, "'Behold now the kindness and the severity of God.' If you are going to know Him more, you are going to know both of these more."

Conviction was coming upon me like a cascade, but it was a cascade of living water. It was cleansing and refreshing, and it was difficult. I also knew that His correction would preserve me through what I was about to encounter after entering through the door. I desperately wanted all of the correction I could get before I entered it. I knew that I would need His correction, and I was right.

Chapter III

the path of life

I was pondering the things that had been spoken by Lot and Jonah when the Lord began to speak.

"You asked to know the reality of this place even as you walk in the earthly realm. This is the reality for which you asked—to see as I see. It is not this place that is the reality. Reality is wherever I am. My presence gives any place true reality and made everything you looked at seem so alive because I am Life. My Father made Me the Life of all creation, both in the heavens and on the earth. All of creation exists through Me and for Me, and apart from Me, there is no life, and there is no truth.

"I am the Life that is in creation. I am even the Life in My enemies. I AM. All that exists does so through Me. I AM the Alpha and the Omega; I AM the Beginning and I AM the End of all things. There is no truth or reality apart from Me. It is not just the reality of this place that you seek, but the reality of My presence. You seek the true knowledge of Me, and this knowledge gives life.

59

This reality is just as available to you in the earthly realm as it is here, but you must learn not to just look for Me, but at Me.

"I am the power of God. I am the revelation of His glory. I am life and I am love. I am also a person. I love My people and want to be with them. The Father loves Me and He also loves you. He loves you so much that He gave Me for your salvation. We want to be close to you. We love mankind and Our eternal dwelling place will be with you. Wisdom is knowing Me, knowing the Father, and knowing Our love. The light, the glory and the power that I am about to reveal in the earth will be released through those who have come to know My love.

"My Father has entrusted Me with all power. I can command the heavens and they obey Me, but I cannot command love. Love commanded is not love at all. There will be a time when I demand obedience from the nations, but then the time to prove your love will have passed. While I am not demanding obedience, those who come to Me obey Me because they love Me and love the truth. These are the ones who will be worthy to reign with Me in My kingdom, those who love Me and serve Me in spite of persecution and rejection. You must want to come to Me. Those who become Our dwelling place will not come because of a command, or just because they know My power—they will come because they love Me and they love the Father.

"Those who come to the truth will come because they love Us and want to be with Us. It is because of the darkness that this is the *age of true love. True love shines the brightest against the greatest darkness. You love Me more when you see Me with your heart and obey Me, even though your eyes cannot see Me as they do now. Love and worship will be greatest in the great darkness that is coming upon the earth. Then all of creation will know that your love for Me is true and why we desire to dwell with men.*

"Those who come to Me now, fighting through all the forces of the world that rebel against Me, come because they have the true love of God. They want to be with Me so much that even when it all seems unreal, even when I seem like a vague dream to them, they will risk all for the hope that the dream is real. That is love. That is the love of the truth. That is the faith that pleases My Father. All will bow the knee when they see My power and glory, but those who bow the knee now when they can only see Me dimly through the eyes of faith are the obedient ones who love Me in Spirit and in truth. These I will soon entrust with the power and glory of the age to come, which is stronger than any darkness.

"As the days grow darker upon the earth, I will show more of My glory. You will need this for what is coming. Even so, remember that those who serve Me even when they do not see My glory are the faithful, obedient ones to whom I will entrust My power. Obedience in the fear of God is the beginning of wisdom, but the fulness of wisdom is to obey because of your love for God. Then you will see the power and the glory.

"You are not here because of your faithfulness. Even the humility that caused you to pray for My judgments was a gift. You are here because you are a messenger. Because I have called you for this purpose, I gave you the wisdom to ask to know My judgments. It is wisdom for you to be faithful to what you see here, but the greatest wisdom is for you to come to Me every day. The more you come to Me, the more real I will be to you. I can be as real to you on the earth as I am to you now, and when you know the reality of My presence, you are walking in truth.

I AM

"Now you see Me as the Lord of Judgment. You must also see Me as the Lord of the Sabbath. I AM both. You must know Me as the Lord of Hosts and behold My armies, and you must see Me as the Prince of Peace. I AM the Lion of Judah, and I AM also the Lamb. To know My wisdom is also to know My times. You are not walking in wisdom if you are proclaiming Me to be the Lion when I want to come as the Lamb. You must know how to follow Me as the Lord of Hosts into battle, and you must know when to sit with Me as the Lord of the Sabbath. To do this, you must know My times, and you can only know My times by staying close to Me.

"The coming judgment for those who call upon My name but do not seek Me will be that they will increasingly fall out of timing with Me. They will be at the wrong place, doing the wrong things, and even preaching the wrong message. They will try to reap when

it is time to sow and sow when it is time to reap. Because of this, they will bear no fruit.

"My name is not *I WAS*, nor is it *I WILL BE*, but *I AM*. To really know Me, you must know Me in the present. You cannot know Me as *I AM* unless you come to Me every day. You cannot know Me as *I AM* unless you abide in Me.

"Here you have had a taste of My judgments. You are about to see Me in other ways. You will not be able to fully know Me as *I AM* until you live in eternity. Here the different aspects of My nature all fit together perfectly, but they are hard to see when you are in the realm of time. This Great Hall reflects a part of Me that the world is about to see. This will be an important part of your message, but it will never be all of it. In one city, I will send My judgment, but in the next I may send mercy. I will send famine to one nation and abundance to another. To know what I am doing, you must not judge by appearances, but from the reality of My presence.

"In the times that are now coming upon the earth, if your love for Me is not growing stronger, it will grow cold. I AM life. If you do not stay close to Me, you will lose the life that is in you. I AM the Light. If you do not stay close to Me, your heart will grow dark.

"All of these things you have known in your mind, and you have taught them. Now you must know them in your heart, and you must live them. The springs of life issue from the heart, not the mind. My wisdom is not just in your mind, nor just in your heart. My *wisdom is the perfect union of both mind and heart. Because man was made in My image, his mind and heart can never agree apart from Me. When your mind and heart agree, I will be able to trust you with My authority. Then you will ask what you will and I will do it because you will be in union with Me.*

"Because of the difficulty of the times in which you are called to walk, I have given you the experience of beholding My Judgment Seat before the appointed time of your judgment. Now your prayer has been answered. What you did not understand was that during the time when you were waiting for Me to answer this prayer, I was answering it every day through all that I allowed to happen in your life.

"It is better to learn of My ways and My judgments through the experiences of life than to learn of them in this way. I have given you this experience because you are a messenger and the time is short. You already knew what you have learned here, but you did not live by that knowledge. I have given you this experience as mercy, but you must choose to live by it.

"I will use many messengers to teach My people to live in righteous judgment so that they do not perish when My judgments come upon the earth. You must hear My messengers and obey their words that are from Me without delay, for the time is now short. To hear them without obeying will only bring a more severe judgment upon you. This is righteous judgment. To whom much is given, much will be required.

"These are the times when knowledge increases. Knowledge of My ways is also increasing with My people. Your generation has been given more understanding than any other generation, but few are living by their understanding. The time has come when I will no longer tolerate those who say they believe Me, but do not obey Me. The lukewarm are about to be removed from among My people. Those who do not obey Me do not really believe in Me. By their lives, they teach My people that disobedience is acceptable.

"As Solomon wrote, 'Because the sentence against an evil deed is not executed quickly, therefore the hearts of the sons of men among them are given fully to do evil.' This has happened to many of My own people, and their love has been growing cold. My judgments are going to come more swiftly as grace to keep My people's hearts from giving themselves fully to evil. They are about to know that the wages of sin is death. They cannot continue to call on Me to deliver them from their troubles when they still love sin. I will give a little more time to judge yourself so that I will not have to judge you, but that time is short.

"Because you have been here, even more will be required of you. I will also impart more grace to you to live by the truth that you know, but you must come to My Throne of Grace every day to get it. I say to you again, the time has come upon the earth when no one will be able to stand in truth without coming to My Throne of Grace each day. What I am about to tell you is so that you and those who are with you cannot only live, but stand and prevail. As My people

stand and prevail over the time of darkness that is coming, the creation will know that light is greater than darkness.

"Life and death have been planted in the earth, and life and death are about to be reaped. I came to give you life. The evil one comes to give death. In the times ahead, both will be seen in their fulness. I will therefore give those who obey Me an abundance of life such as has never been seen on earth before. There will be a distinction between My people and those who serve the evil one. Choose life that you may live. Choose life by obeying Me. If you are choosing Me and the light that is in you is My true light, it will grow brighter every day. By this you will know that you are walking in My light. The seed that is planted in good soil always grows and multiplies: You will be known by your fruit."

CHAPTER IV

truth and life

As the Lord spoke, His glory seemed to increase. It was so great that at times, I thought I was going to be consumed by it. His glory burned, but it was not like a fire; it burned from the inside out. I somehow knew that I would either be consumed by His glory or by the evil I would face after I went through the door. His words were penetrating and gripping, but I knew that it was even more important to behold His glory, so I was determined to do just that for as long as I could.

He appeared more brilliant than the sun. I could not see all of His features because of the brightness, but as I continued to look, my eyes adjusted some to His brilliance. His eyes were like fire, but not red; they were blue, like the hottest part of the fire. They were fierce, yet had the attraction of an endless wonder.

His hair was black and sparkled with what I thought at first were stars, and then I realized that it glistened with oil.

I knew that this was the oil of unity, which I had seen in a vision before. This oil radiates like precious stones, but is more beautiful and more valuable than any earthly treasure. As I looked at His face, I felt the oil begin to cover me, and as it did, the pain of the fire of His glory was more bearable. It seemed to impart peace and rest, and only came upon me as I looked at His face. When I looked away from His face, it would stop.

I felt compelled to look at His feet. They also were like flames of fire, but were more of a bronze or golden flame. They were beautiful, but also fearsome, as if they were about to walk with the most fearful of strides. As I looked at His feet, I felt like an earthquake was going off inside of me, and I knew that as He walked, everything that could be shaken would be shaken. I could only stand it for a moment, and then I had to fall on my face.

When I looked up, I was looking at the door. Now it was even less attractive than before. At the same time, I felt a desperation to go through it before I would choose not to. It was my calling to go through the door, and to not go would be to not obey. In His presence, even the *thought* of disobedience seemed to be such a base selfishness more repulsive than the thought of returning to the battle of the earthly realm.

As I looked at the door, I heard another voice begin to speak which I did not recognize. I turned to see who was speaking. He was one of the most naturally attractive people I had seen yet, regal and strong.

"I am Abel," he said. "The authority that the Lord is about to give His people is the anointing for true unity. When there were just two brothers on the earth, we could not live in peace with one another. From my time until yours, mankind has walked in the way of increasing darkness. Murder will be released on the earth as never before. Even your World Wars were but birth pangs leading to what is to come. But remember this: Love is stronger than death. The love that the Father is about to give to those who serve Him will overcome death."

"Please, tell me everything that you have been given to tell me," I responded, knowing that he had much to say.

"My blood still speaks. The blood of every martyr still speaks. Your message will live on if you trust in the life that you have in God more than you trust in the life that you have on earth. Do not fear death, and you will overcome it. Those who do not fear death will have the greatest message during the times you are entering when death is released on the earth.

I thought of all of the wars, famines and plagues that had come upon the earth just in my century. "How much more can death be released?" I asked.

Abel continued without answering me, which I understood to be the answer. "The blood sacrifice has already been made for you. Trust the power of the cross, for it is greater than life. When you trust the cross, you cannot die. Those on earth have power for a time to take your earthly life, but they cannot take your life if you have embraced the cross.

"A great unity will come to the Lord's people who dwell on the earth. This will take place when His judgments come upon the earth. Those who are in unity will not only endure His judgments, but they will prosper because of them. By this He will use His people to warn the earth. After the warnings, He will then use His people as a sign. Because of the discord and conflict that arise in the darkness, the unity of His people will be a sign that the whole earth will see. His disciples will be known by their love, and love does not fear. Only true love can bring true unity. Those who love will never fall. True love does not grow cold, but true love does grow."

Love Releases Life

Another man who looked almost exactly like Abel came and stood beside him.

"I am Adam," he said. "I was given authority over the earth, but I gave it to the evil one by obeying evil. He now rules in my place and your place. The earth was given to man, but the evil one has taken it. The authority I lost was restored by the cross. Jesus Christ is 'the last Adam,' and He will soon take His authority and rule. He will rule through mankind because He gave the earth to mankind. Those who live in your times will prepare the earth for Him to rule."

"Please tell me more," I asked, a little surprised to see Adam, but wanting to hear everything he had to say. "How do we prepare for Him?"

"Love," he said. "You must love one another. You must love the earth, and you must love life. My sin released the death that now flows as rivers upon the earth. Your love will release rivers of life. When evil reigns, death is stronger than life, and death prevails over life. When righteousness reigns, life prevails, and life is stronger than death. Soon the life of the Son of God will swallow up the death that was released through my disobedience. It is not just living that you must love, but *life*. Death is your enemy. You are called to be a messenger of life.

"When the Lord's people begin to love, He will use them to release His judgments. His judgments are to be desired. The whole world is groaning and travailing as it waits for His judgments, and when they come, the world will learn righteousness. What He is about to do, He will do through His people, and His people will stand as Elijah in the last days. Their words will shut up the heavens or bring rain; they will prophesy earthquakes and famines, and they will come to pass; they will stop famines and earthquakes.

"When they release armies in the heavens, armies will march on the earth. When they hold back armies, there will be peace. They will decide where He shows mercy and where He shows His wrath. They will have this authority because they will love, and those who love will be one with Him. What you will see through that door is to help prepare you for what He is about to do through His people.

"I know authority. I also know the responsibility of authority. Because of the great authority that I was given, I am responsible for what has happened to the earth. Even so, the grace of God began to cover me, and God's great redemption will soon swallow up my mistake. Peace will be taken from the earth, but you are called to help restore it. Peace prevails in heaven, and you are called to bring heaven to earth. Those who abide in His presence will know peace and will spread peace.

"The earth itself will shake and tremble. Times of trouble greater than have ever been known will begin to move across the earth like great waves of the sea. Even so, those who know Him will not be troubled. They will stand before the raging of the seas and say, 'Peace, be still' and the seas will be calm. Even the least of His little ones will be like a great fortress of peace that will stand through all that is coming. His glory will be revealed to His people first and then through them. Even the creation will recognize Him in His people and will obey them as it does Him.

"This is the authority that I had, and it will be given to mankind again. I used my authority to turn Paradise into a wilderness. The Lord will use His authority to turn the wilderness into Paradise again. This is the authority that He is giving to His people. I used mine wrongly and death came. When His authority is used in righteousness, it will release life. Be careful how you use authority. With authority comes responsibility. You, too, can use it wrongly, but you will not do this if you love. As all of heaven knows, 'Love never fails.'"

"What about the earthquakes, famines and even wars that you said we would release on the earth? Won't this be releasing death?" I asked.

"All the death that is coming upon the world is being allowed to prepare the way for life. Everything that is sown must be reaped, unless those who have sown evil call upon the cross in Spirit and truth. The army of the cross is about to be released, and it will march in the power of the cross, carrying the offer of mercy to all. Those who reject the mercy of God have rejected life."

"That is a great responsibility," I said. "How do we know when they have rejected His mercy?"

"Disobedience brought death, and obedience will bring life. When I walked with God, He taught me His ways. As I walked with Him, I began to know Him. You must walk with God and learn of His ways. Your authority is His authority, and you must be one with Him in order to use it. The weapons of His army are not carnal—they are spiritual and much more powerful than any earthly weapons. Your most powerful weapons are truth and love. Even the final judgment of destruction is God's love extended in mercy.

"When truth spoken in love is rejected, death has been chosen over life. You will understand this as you walk with Him. You will come to understand the Spirit that He has given to you to bring life and not death. There is a time to give men over to reap what they have sown, but you must do all things in obedience. Jesus came to give *life*. He does not desire for any to perish, and this must be your desire also. For this reason, you must even love your enemies if you are to be trusted with the authority that He wants to give to His people.

"The time is at hand for the fulfillment of what has been written. His people have prayed for more time, and He gave it to them. However, few have used it wisely. You have a little more time, but soon the time can no longer be delayed. The time is near when time itself will seem to speed up. As it is written, when He comes, He will come quickly. However, you are not to fear the times. If you fear Him, you do not need to fear anything that is coming upon the earth.

"All that is about to happen is coming so that His wisdom can again prevail on earth just as it does in heaven. All of the evil that was sown in mankind is about to be reaped. Even so, the good that He has sown will also be reaped. Goodness is stronger than evil. Love is stronger than death. He walked the earth to destroy the works of the devil, and He will finish what He has begun."

Power and Love

As Adam talked, I was captured by his grace and dignity. I began to wonder if he had possibly lived his whole life after the fall without sinning again because he seemed to be so pure. Knowing my thoughts, he changed the subject briefly to answer them.

"I lived long on the earth because sin did not have a deep root in me. Even though I had sinned, I was created to walk with God, and my desire was still for Him. I did not know the depths of sin that the following generations knew. As sin grew, life was shortened, but in every generation, those who walk with God touch the life that is in God. Because Moses walked so closely with God, he would have lived on had the Lord not taken him. Enoch walked with Him so closely that the Lord had to take him as well. That is why Jesus said, 'I am the resurrection and the life; he who believes in Me shall live even if he dies, and everyone who lives and believes in Me shall never die.'

"What you are seeing in me is not just the lack of sin, but the presence of life that I had on the earth. What we were on earth will remain a part of who we are forever. I can look at all of the others here who are a part of the great cloud of witnesses and know much about their life on earth."

"So you are a part of the great cloud of witnesses."

"Yes. My story is a part of the eternal gospel. My wife and I were the first to taste sin, and the first to see our children reap the consequences of disobedience. We have beheld the death spread through each generation, but we have also beheld the cross and seen the victory over sin.

"Satan has boasted since the cross that Jesus could *redeem* men but could not *change* them. During the times of the greatest darkness and evil that are about to come, His people will stand as a testimony for all time that He not only redeemed His people from sin, but He also removed sin from them. Through them, He will remove sin from the whole earth. He will now display to the whole creation the power of His new creation. He did not come just to forgive sin, but to save mankind from sin, and He is returning for a people who are without stain from the world. This will come to pass in the most difficult of times.

"I was created to love the Lord and to love the earth, as were all people. I have loathed the sight of the world's rivers becoming sewers. Even more have I loathed the sight of what has happened to the human mind. The philosophies of the human mind now filling the streams of human thought are as loathsome as the sewage filling the rivers. But the rivers of human thought will one day be pure again, just as the rivers of the earth. By this, for all time to come, it will be proven that good is stronger than evil.

"The Lord did not go to the cross just to redeem, but also to restore. He walked the earth as a man to show mankind how to live. He will now reveal Himself through His chosen ones to show them who they were created to be. This demonstration will not just come through power, but through love. He will give you power because He is all powerful, and power is also a revelation of Him. Even so, He uses His power because of love and so must you. Even His judgments come because of love. When you send them forth, it must be because of love. Even His final judgment of the earth will be His final mercy."

I looked at Adam, Abel, Lot and Jonah as they stood together. I knew that it would take forever to understand the depths of the revelation of the great gospel of God that each of their lives represented. Adam's disobedience made the way for Abel's obedience, whose blood still speaks as a harbinger of salvation. Righteous Lot could not save a city, while an unrighteous Jonah could. Like the four gospels, there seemed to be no end to the understanding that could be learned from them. This, too, was my call.

CHAPTER V

the DOOR

I tried desperately to absorb every word these men had spoken to me. Never had Wisdom said so much to me at once, yet I felt that every sentence was crucial, and I did not want to forget anything. I thought about how good it would be to have His words carved in stone like Moses and to carry the words of the Lord to His people in such a way that they could be preserved untainted by me. Again knowing my thoughts, Wisdom answered them.

"That is the difference between the Old Covenant and the New. You will write My words in a book and they will inspire My people. Even so, the true power of My words can only be seen when they are written in the hearts of My people. Living epistles are more powerful than letters written on paper or stone. Because you are not writing Scripture, the words you write will have you in them. Even so, your books will be as I desire them to be because I prepared you for this task. They will not be perfect because perfection will not

come to the earth until I come. For perfection, men will have to look to me. Even so, My people are the book that I am writing, and the wise can see Me in My people, and in their works.

"My Father sent Me into the world because He loves the world, and I am sending My people into the world because I love the world. I could have judged the world after My resurrection, but the course of the world was allowed to continue so that My righteous ones could be proven and the power of what I did on the cross would be seen in mankind. I did this because of love. You are the witnesses of My love. This is My commandment to you: Love Me and love your neighbor. Only then will your witness be true. Even when I command you to speak of My judgments, it must be in love.

"The life of every person is in My book, and their lives are a book that will be read by all of creation for all eternity. The history of the world is the library of God's Wisdom. My redemption is the demonstration of Our love, and the cross is the greatest love that the creation will ever know. Even the angels who stand before My Father so love the story of redemption that they, too, long to dwell with men. They marveled when We made man in our image. They marveled when men chose evil, even in the midst of the Paradise We had made for man. Now, because of redemption, the marred image of God is restored and is revealed even more gloriously in mankind. The glory is still in earthen vessels which makes the glory easier to see for those who have eyes to see.

"This is the new creation that is greater than the first creation. Through My new creation, we are making a new Paradise that is greater than the first Paradise. Every man, woman and child that embraces My redemption is a book that I am writing which will be read forever. Through the new creation, We will also restore the former creation, and it will be a paradise again. I will restore all things, and all evil will be overcome with good.

"My church is the book that I am writing, and the whole world is about to read it. Until now, the world has wanted to read the book that the evil one has written about My church, but soon I will release My book.

"I am about to release My last-day apostles. I will have many like Paul, John, Peter and the others. To prepare them, I am sending many like John the Baptist who will teach them devotion to Me and lay the foundation of repentance in their lives. These apostles will also be like John the Baptist. Just as the chief joy of John's life was to hear the voice of the Bridegroom, these will have one devotion— to see My bride made ready for Me. Because of this, I will use them to build highways through the wilderness and rivers through the deserts. They will bring down the high places and raise up the lowly. When you go through that door, you will meet them.

"I am about to release My last-day prophets. They will love Me and walk with Me, even as Enoch did. They will demonstrate My power and prove to the world that I am the One true God. Each will be a pure well from which only living waters flow. At times, *their water will be hot for cleansing; at times, it will be cold for refreshing. I will also give them lightening in one hand and thunder in the other. They will soar like eagles over the earth, but they will descend upon My people like doves because they will honor My family. They will come upon cities like whirlwinds and earthquakes, but they will give light to the meek and lowly. When you go through that door, you will also meet them.*

"I am about to release My last-day evangelists. I will give them a cup of joy that will never run out. They will heal the sick and cast out devils; they will love Me and love righteousness; they will carry their crosses every day, not living for themselves but for Me. Through them, the world will know that I live and that I have been given all authority and power. These are the fearless ones who will attack the gates of the enemy and raid the dark places of the earth, leading many to My salvation. These, too, are just beyond that door, and you will meet them.

"I am about to release shepherds who will have My heart for the sheep. These will feed My sheep because they love Me. They will care for each of My little ones as if they were their own, and they will lay down their own lives for My sheep. This is the love that will touch men's hearts—when My people lay down their lives for one another. Then the world will know Me. I have given these choice food to serve My household. These are the faithful ones that I will trust to watch over My own house. These, too, are beyond that door, and you will meet them.

"I am about to release My last-day teachers upon the earth. They will know Me and teach My people to know Me. They will love the truth. They will not retreat before the darkness, but they will expose it and drive it back. They will unstop the wells that your fathers dug, and serve the pure waters of life. They will also carry out the treasures of Egypt and use it to build My dwelling place. You will meet these, too, just beyond that door."

As the Lord spoke, I looked at the door. Now, for the first time, I wanted to go through it. Each word that He spoke brought a rising expectation in my heart, and I badly wanted to meet these last-day ministers.

"You have known in your heart for many years that these are coming. I have brought you here to show you how to recognize them and help them on their way."

I went through the door.

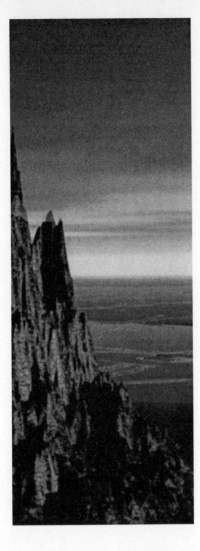

CHAPTER VI

the príson

Suddenly, I was standing in a large prison yard. There were huge walls such as I had never seen before. They extended for as far as I could see, hundreds of feet high and very thick. There were other fences and razor wire in front of the wall. Every few hundred feet there were guard towers along the top of the wall. I could see guards in each one, but they were too far away for me to see much about them.

It was grey, dark and dreary, which seemed to perfectly reflect the mass of people who stood in the prison yard. All over the yard, people sat in groups of their own kind. Old black men were in one group, young black men in another. Old and young white men also stayed apart, and the women were also separated. With every race, this seemed to be the same. Those with any distinguishing characteristic were separated, except for the youngest children.

Between the groups, many people seemed to be milling around. As I watched, I could tell that they were trying to find their own identity by finding the group which they were the most like. However, it was obvious that these groups did not let anyone join them easily.

As I looked more closely at these people, I could see that they all had deep wounds and many scars from previous wounds. Except for the children, they all seemed to be nearly blind and could only see well enough to stay in their own group. Even within their groups, they were constantly trying to see the differences that others might have. When they found even a small difference, they would attack the one who was different. They all seemed hungry, thirsty and sick.

I approached an older man and asked him why they were all in prison. He looked at me in astonishment, declaring emphatically that they were not in prison, and why would I ask such a stupid thing. I pointed at the fences and the guards, and he replied, "What fences? What guards?" He looked at me as if I had insulted him terribly, and I knew that if I asked him anything else, I would be attacked.

I asked a young woman the same question and received the same response. I then realized that they were so blind that they could not even see the fences or the guards. These people did not know that they were in prison.

The Guard

I decided to ask a guard why these people were in prison. As I walked toward the fences, I could see holes in them that would be easy to climb through. When I reached the wall itself, I found it so irregularly built that it was easy for me to climb. Anyone could easily escape, but no one was trying because they did not know that they were captives.

When I got to the top of the wall, I could see for a great distance and saw the sun shining beyond the walls. It did not shine in the prison yard because of the height of the wall and the clouds that hung over it. I saw fires far off in the prison yard toward the end where the children were gathered. The smoke from these fires formed a thick cloud over the yard that turned what would have been just shade from the walls into a choking, dreary haze. I wondered what was burning.

I walked along the top of the wall until I reached the guard post. I was surprised to find the guard dressed in a fine suit with a collar indicating that he was some kind of minister or priest. He was not shocked to see me, and I think he assumed that I was another guard.

"Sir, why are these people in prison?" I asked.

That question shocked him, and I watched fear and suspicion come over him like a blanket.

"What prison?" he replied. "What are you talking about?"

"I am talking about those people in this prison yard," I said, feeling a strange boldness. "You're obviously a prison guard because you're in a guard house, but why are you dressed like that?" I continued.

"I am not a prison guard! I am a minister of the gospel. I am not their guard—I am their spiritual leader. This is not a guard house—it is the Lord's house! Son, if you think your questions are funny, I am not laughing!" He grabbed his gun and seemed ready to shoot at me.

"Please excuse me for disturbing you," I replied, sensing that he would definitely use his gun.

As I walked away, I expected to hear shots at any moment. The man was so insecure I knew he would shoot before thinking if he felt threatened. I could also tell that he was sincere. He really did not know that he was a guard.

The School Teacher

I walked along the wall until I felt I was a safe distance away and turned to look back at the minister. He was pacing back and forth in his guardhouse, greatly agitated. I wondered why my questions disturbed him so much. It was obvious that my questions did not open him to seeing anything differently, but rather made him even more insecure and more deadly.

As I walked, I felt a desperation to find out what was going on and I thought about how I could rephrase my questions so as not to offend the next guard I tried to talk to. As I approached the next guard house, I was again surprised by the appearance of the guard. It was not another minister, but a young lady who was about 25 years old.

"Miss, may I ask you some questions?" I inquired.

"Certainly. What can I help you with?" she said with a condescending air. "Are you the parent of one of these children?"

"No," I responded. "I am a writer," which I somehow knew was the answer I should give her. As I expected, this got her attention.

Not wanting to make the same mistake I had made with the minister by calling what he was standing in a "guard house," I asked the young lady why she was standing in "that place." Her response was immediate, and she seemed surprised that I did not know.

"I'm a school teacher, so don't you think it quite natural that I should be in my school?"

"So this is your *school*," I replied, indicating the guard house.

"Yes. I've been here for three years now. I may be here the rest of my life. I love what I'm doing so much." This last remark was so mechanical that I knew I would discover something if I pressed her.

"What do you teach? It must be interesting for you to consider spending the rest of your life doing it."

"I teach general science and social studies. It is my job to shape the philosophy and world view of these young minds. What I teach them will steer them for the rest of their lives. What do you write?" she inquired.

"Books," I responded, "I write leadership books," anticipating her next question. I also somehow knew that if I had said, "*Christian* leadership books," our conversation would have ended. She seemed even more interested after this answer.

"Leadership is an important subject," she stated, still with a slightly condescending air. "Changes are happening so quickly that we must have the right leadership tools to steer these changes in the right direction."

"What direction is that?" I asked.

"Toward the prosperity that can only come through peace and security," she replied, as if she were surprised that I would even ask such a question.

"I don't mean to offend you," I replied, "but I'm interested in your views on this. What do you feel is the best way for this peace and security to be achieved?"

"Through education of course. We are together on this spaceship earth and we have to get along. Through education, we are helping deliver the masses from their caveman, tribal mentality to understand that we are all the same and that if we all do our part for society, we will all prosper together."

"That's interesting," I replied, "but we are not all the same. It is also interesting that all of the people down there are becoming even more divided and separated than ever. Do you think that it may be time to possibly modify your philosophy a bit?"

She looked at me in both amazement and agitation, but obviously not because she even considered for a moment that what I said was true.

"Sir, are you completely blind?" she finally responded.

"No, I believe I see quite well," I answered. "I have just come from walking among the people and have never seen such division and animosity between different people groups. It seems to me that the conflict between them is worse than ever."

I could tell that my statements were like slaps in the face to this young lady. It was as if she just could not believe someone was even saying these things, much less believing that there was a chance there might be some truth to them. As I watched her, I could tell that she was so blind that she could barely see me. She was in such a high tower that there was no way that she could see the people below. She really did not know what was going on, but sincerely thought that she could see everything.

"We are changing the world," she said with obvious disdain. "We are changing people. If there are still people acting like beasts such as you described, we will change them, too. We will prevail. Mankind will prevail."

"That is quite a responsibility for someone so young," I remarked.

She bristled even more at that statement, but before she could respond, two women appeared walking toward the door of the guard house along the top of the wall. One was a black woman who appeared to be in her fifties and the other was a very well-dressed white woman who was probably in her early thirties. They talked with each other as they walked, and both appeared confident and dignified. I could tell that they could see, which is obviously how they reached the top of the wall.

To my surprise, the young school teacher grabbed her gun and stepped outside of the guardhouse to meet them, obviously not wanting these women to get any closer. She greeted them with a very superficial cheerfulness and an obvious air of superiority that she seemed to want to impress on them. To my surprise, the two women became timid and overly respectful of one who was so much younger.

"We've come to ask about something our children are being taught that we do not understand," the black woman stated, mustering some courage.

"Oh, I'm sure that a lot is now taught that you do not understand," the teacher replied condescendingly.

The women kept looking at the teacher's gun which she handled in such a way so that they would constantly be aware of it. I was standing close by, amazed by this whole scene. The teacher turned and looked at me nervously. I could tell that she was afraid I might say something to the women. As she fingered the gun, she demanded that I leave. The women looked up to see to whom she was talking, and I realized that they could not see me. Their fear had blinded them.

I called out to the women, entreating them to have courage and believe what they felt in their heart. They looked in my direction as if they could only hear noise. They were losing their ability to hear as well. Seeing this, the young teacher smiled. She then aimed her gun at me and blew a whistle. I felt as if she perceived me to be the most dangerous person alive.

I knew that I could not wait for whoever she had called with her whistle. I also realized that if I just stepped back a little, I would be safe because this young teacher was so blind. I was right. I walked away with her screaming, blowing her whistle, and finally becoming so enraged that she began to shoot at the two women.

As I stood on top of the wall between two guard posts wondering about all of this, I felt the presence of Wisdom.

"You must return to the prison yard. I will be with you. Know that you have the vision to escape any trap or weapon. Only

remember that fear can blind you. As you walk in the faith that I am with you, you will always see the way to go. You must also be careful to only reveal your vision to those to whom I lead you. Vision is what the guards fear the most. I know you want to ask me a lot of questions, but they will be better answered by the experiences you will have there."

CHAPTER VII

the young apostle

I climbed down and began to walk through the yard. As I passed by the prisoners, they seemed almost completely disinterested in me or all of the commotion on the wall. I then remembered that they could not see that far. A young black man stepped into my path and looked at me with bright, inquisitive eyes.

"Who are you?" we both said at the same time.

As we stood looking at each other, he finally said, "My name is Stephen. I can see. What else do you want to know about me that you do not already know?"

"How could I know anything else about you?" I inquired.

"The one who helped me to see said that one day, others would come who were not prisoners. They would also be able to see, and they would tell us who we are and how we can escape from this prison."

I started to protest that I did not know who he was when I remembered what Wisdom had told me about those whom I would meet when I passed through the next door.

"I do know you, and I know some things about you," I acknowledged, "But I confess that this is the weirdest prison I have ever seen."

"But this is the only prison!" he protested.

"How do you know that if you have been here all of your life?" I asked.

"The one who helped me to see told me that it was the only one. He said that every soul who had ever been imprisoned was held captive here. He always told me the truth, so I believe this."

"Who is the one who helped you to see?" I asked, not only wanting to know who had helped him to see, but also interested in how this was the prison that held every soul captive.

"He never told me his real name, but just called Himself 'Wisdom.'"

"Wisdom! What did He look like?" I questioned.

"He was a young, black athlete. He could see better than anyone and seemed to know everyone here. It is strange, though. I have met others here who said that they have also met Wisdom, but they all described Him differently. Some said that He was white and others said that He was a woman. Unless there are many 'Wisdoms,' He is a master of disguise."

"Can you take me to Him?" I asked.

"I would, but I have not seen Him for a long time now. I am afraid that He has left or maybe even died. I have been very discouraged since He departed. My vision even started getting worse until I saw you. As soon as I saw you, I knew that everything He told me was true. He said that you knew Him, too, so why are you asking me so much about Him?"

"I do know Him! And be encouraged, your Friend is not dead. I will tell you His real name, too, but first I must ask you a few questions."

"I know that you can be trusted, and I know that you and others like you who are coming will want to meet everyone who can see. I can take you to some of them. I also know that you and the others are coming to help a lot of these other prisoners to see. I am surprised by one thing though."

"What is that?"

"You are white. I never thought that the ones who came to help us see and be set free would be white."

"I am sure that there are many others coming who are not white," I responded. "I can tell that you already have considerable vision, so I know you can understand what I am about to say."

The Value of Vision

As I looked at Stephen to be sure he was listening, I was moved by how open and teachable he was, in striking contrast to the teacher who had been about his same age. This man will be a true teacher, I thought as I continued.

"When we get to the place of ultimate vision, we will not judge people by the color of their skin, gender or age. We will not judge others by appearances, but after the spirit."

"That sounds like what our teachers used to tell us," Stephen responded, a little surprised.

"There is a difference though," I continued. "They tried to make you think that we are all alike, but we were created different for a reason. True peace will only come when we respect the distinctions we have. When we really know who we are, we will never be threatened by those who are different. When we are free, we are free to show those who are different from us honor and respect, always seeking to learn from one another, just as you are now doing with me."

"I understand," Stephen replied. "I hope I didn't offend you by saying that I was surprised that you were white."

"No, I was not offended. I understand. I am encouraged that you were able to recognize me in spite of the color of my skin. But remember, every time we open our hearts to learn

106

from those who are different, our vision will increase. Your eyes are already brighter than when we first met."

"I was just thinking about how quickly my vision is being restored," Stephen remarked.

"I now know why I am here." I added, "You must keep in mind that your vision is your most valuable possession. Every day you must do that which will help to increase your vision. Stay away from the people and things that make you lose your vision."

"Yes, like getting discouraged."

"Exactly! Discouragement is usually the beginning of the loss of vision," I said. "To accomplish our purposes, we must resist discouragement in any form. Discouragement blinds."

"When I began to see, I started to feel that I had a purpose, maybe even an important one," Stephen continued. "Can you help me to know what my purpose is?"

"Yes, I think I can. To know our purpose is one of the greatest ways that our vision grows. It is also one of our greatest defenses against things like discouragement which destroys vision. I think my main purpose here is to help you and the others whose vision is being restored to know their purpose. But first we need to talk about something even more important."

Buried Treasure

When Stephen spoke, I could hear the voice of Wisdom, so I knew that this young man had been taught by the Lord. I also knew that he did not know the Lord's name and would have difficulty believing that Wisdom's name was Jesus. I knew that I would need wisdom just to share the name of Wisdom. I thought about the apostles, prophets, evangelists, pastors and teachers that Wisdom said I would meet when I went through the door. I never dreamed that I would meet them in a place like this. As I looked out over the great mass of people, I felt His presence. He was with me and even in the gloom of this terrible prison, excitement was welling up in me. This is what I have been prepared for, I thought.

"Stephen, what do you see when you look at this great mass of people?" I asked.

"I see confusion, despair, bitterness, hatred. I see darkness," he replied.

"That is certainly true, but look again with the eyes of your heart. Use your vision," I responded.

He looked for a long time and then said with some hesitation, "I now see a great field with buried treasure in it. The treasure is everywhere and in almost every form."

"That is right," I responded. "This is also a revelation of your purpose. You are a treasure hunter. Some of the greatest souls who ever lived are trapped here, and you will help find them and set them free."

"But how will I find them, and how will I set them free when I am not even free?"

"You already know how to find them, but it is true that you will not be able to set them free until you are free. That is your next lesson. You must also remember that you will always know your purpose in a situation by seeing with the eyes of your heart. What you see from your innermost being will always reveal your purpose."

"Is that how you knew I am to be a treasure hunter?"

"Yes. But you must be free before you can become who you were created to be. Why haven't you escaped through those holes in the fence?" I asked.

"When I first began to see, I saw the fences and the wall. I also saw the holes in the fences and have gone through them. When I got to the wall, I tried several times to climb it, but fear would overcome me because I am afraid of heights. I also thought that if I got over the wall, I would be shot."

"Those guards cannot see nearly as well as you think," I replied. "They are almost as blind as the people here."

This seemed to really surprise Stephen, but I could also tell that it opened his eyes even more.

"Can you see the top of the wall?" I asked.

"Yes, I can see it from here."

"I want you to remember this," I continued. "I have now been in many places. Call them different worlds, or realms, if you will. There is one important principle that I have found to be true in every place, and you must remember it for the rest of your life."

"What is it?"

"You can always go as far as you can see. If you can see the top of the wall, you can get there. When you get to the top of the wall, you will be able to see farther than you have ever seen before. You must keep going for as far as you can see. Never stop as long as you can still see farther."

"I understand," he replied immediately. "But I'm still afraid to climb that wall. It's so high! Is it safe?"

"I will not lie to you and tell you it is safe, but I know that it is much more dangerous *not* to climb it. If you do not use your vision by walking in what you see, you will lose it. Then you will perish here."

"How will I seek out the treasure that is here if I leave?"

"That is a good question, but it is also one which keeps many from fulfilling their purpose. I can only tell you now that you have a great journey you must complete first. At the end of your journey, you will find a door leading you back to this prison, just as I found. When you return, your vision will be so great that they will never be able to trap you here again. Your vision will also be great enough to see the treasure that is here."

CHAPTER VIII

the light

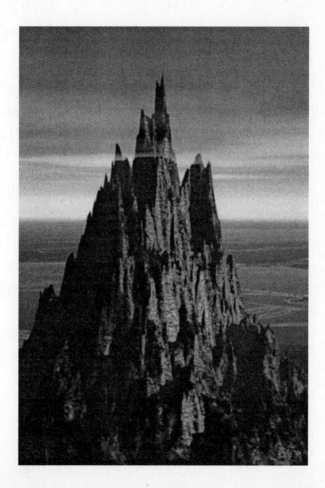

Stephen turned and looked again at the wall. "I still feel great fear," he lamented. "I don't know if I can do it."

"You have vision, but you lack faith. Vision and faith must work together," I said. "There is a reason why your faith is weak."

"Please tell me what it is! Is there something that will help my faith to grow as my vision increases?"

"Yes. Faith comes from knowing who Wisdom really is. You must know His true name. Just knowing His name will give you enough faith to get you over that wall to freedom. The better you get to know His name, the greater the obstacles and barriers you will be able to overcome on your journey. One day you will know His name well enough to move any mountain."

"What is His name?" Stephen almost begged.

"His name is Jesus."

Stephen looked at the ground, and then up in the air as disbelief seemed to come over him. I watched as the struggle went on between his heart and his mind. Finally he looked at me again, and to my great relief, he still had hope in his eyes. I knew that he had listened to his heart.

"I suspected it," he said. "In fact, the whole time you were talking, I somehow knew that you were going to say that. I also know that you are telling me the truth. But I have some questions. Can I ask them?"

"Of course."

"I have known many people who use the name of Jesus, but they are not free. In fact, they are some of the most bound people that I know here. Why?"

"That is a good question, and I can only tell you what I have learned on my own journey. I think that every case is different, but there are many who know His name, but do not know *Him*. Instead of drawing closer to Him and being changed by seeing Him as He is, they try to make Him into their image. Knowing the name of Jesus is much more than just knowing how to spell it or say it. It is knowing who He really is. This is where true faith comes from."

I could still see doubt in Stephen's eyes, but it was the good kind of doubt—the kind that wants to believe rather than the kind that wants to disbelieve. I continued.

"There are others who really love Jesus and start to sincerely get to know Him, but they also remain prisoners. These are the ones who let the wounds or mistakes suffered on the journey turn them back. These have tasted freedom, but they returned to prison because of disappointments or failures. You can easily recognize them because they are always talking about the past instead of the future. If they were still walking by their vision, they would not always be looking backward."

"I have met many of those," Stephen remarked.

"You need to understand something if you are ever going to have this question answered. If you are to fulfill your destiny, you cannot be overly discouraged or encouraged by others who use the name of Jesus. We are not called to place our faith in His people, but in Him. Even the greatest souls will disappoint us at times because they are still human.

"Many who are like those I just described can also become great souls. Vision and faith can be restored, even in those who have become the most discouraged and disappointed. As a treasure hunter, this is your job. We cannot discard any human being—they are all treasures to Him. However, to really know Him and walk in true faith, you must not judge Him by His people, either the best or the worst," I shared.

"I always thought of Jesus as the white man's God. He never seemed to do much for our people."

"He is not a white man's God—He was not even white Himself! But neither is He a black man's God. He created all and He is the Lord of all. When you start to see Him as the God of any one group, you have greatly reduced who He is, and you have greatly reduced your own vision."

Faith and Obedience

I watched silently as Stephen wrestled with many other things in his heart. I continued to feel the presence of Wisdom, and I knew that He could explain all things much better than I could. Finally Stephen looked up at me, with the light shining brighter than ever in his eyes.

"I know that all of the questions that I have been wrestling with really do not have anything to do with who Jesus really is, but who people have said He is. I know what you are saying is true. I know that Jesus is the One who gave me vision and that He is Wisdom; I must find out for myself who He really is; I must seek Him; I must serve Him. I also know that He has sent you here to help me get started. What do I do?"

"Wisdom is here now," I began. "You heard Him when I spoke, just as I heard Him speaking through you. You already know His voice. He is your Teacher. He will speak to you through many different people, sometimes even through those who do not know Him. Be quick to hear and obey what He says. Faith and obedience are the same. You do not have true faith if you do not obey, and if you have true faith you will always obey.

"You said that you will serve Him. That means that you will no longer live for yourself, but for Him. In the presence of Wisdom, you know the difference between what is right and what is wrong. When you come to know Wisdom, you will also understand what is evil. You must renounce the evil that you have done in the past, as well as that which comes to tempt you in the future.

"You cannot live as others do. You are called to be a soldier of the cross. When you embraced His name and the truth of who He is; when that great light came into your eyes; when the peace and satisfaction began to flood your soul just a few moments ago, you were born again and began a new life. Wisdom has been speaking to you for sometime, guiding you and teaching you, but now He lives *in* you. He will never leave you again. But He is not your servant, you are His."

"I do feel Him!" Stephen acknowledged. "But how I would love to see Him again!"

"You can see Him with the eyes of your heart at any time. This is also your call—to see Him more clearly and to follow Him more closely. That is what the journey is for. On your journey, you will learn about His name, and the power of the cross. When you have been trained, you will return here in that power, and you will help to set many of these captives free."

"Will you still be here?"

"I do not know. Sometimes I will have work to do here, and sometimes I will have work to do helping others on their journeys. I might meet you again out there where you are going. I am also still on my own journey. This is part of it. On your journey, there will be many doors that you must go through. You never know where they will lead. Some may bring you back here. Some doors may take you into the wilderness which all must travel through. Some lead to glorious heavenly experiences, and it is tempting to always look for those doors, but they are not always the ones we need to help us fulfill our destiny. Do not choose doors by their appearance, but always ask Wisdom to help you."

Stephen turned his gaze upon the wall. I watched a smile appear.

"I can climb that wall now," he said. "I even look forward to the challenge. I must admit that I still feel the fear, but it does not matter. I know that I can climb it, and I cannot wait to see what is behind it. I know that I am free. I am no longer a prisoner!"

I walked with Stephen to the first fence. He was surprised to discover that there were not only holes in it, but that wherever he touched them, the fences would fall apart in his hand, making other holes.

"What are these fences made of?" he asked.

"Delusions," I explained. "Every time someone escapes through them, a hole is made for others to go through. You can go through the holes that are already here or make one yourself."

Stephen chose a place that was thick with barbed wire, stretched out his arms and walked straight into it, opening a large hole as he went. I knew that he would one day return here and lead many others out through the hole he was now making. Watching him was sheer joy. I felt the presence of Wisdom so strongly that I knew I would see Him if I turned around. I did, and I was right. The great joy I was experiencing could be seen on His face as well.

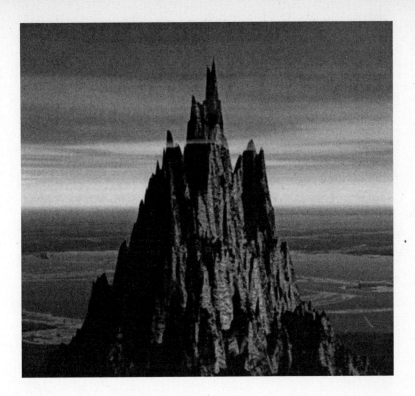

CHAPTER IX

FREEDOM

As I stood next to Wisdom watching Stephen walk through the fences, he called out, "What is the wall made of?"

"Fear."

I watched Stephen stop and look at the wall. It was huge. Many never got past the fences, and I knew that this was a crucial test for Stephen.

Without looking back, he called out again, "Will you help me climb it?"

"I can't help you," I responded. "If I try to help you, it will only take you twice as long and be even harder. To conquer your fears, you must face them alone."

"The more I look up at it the worse it seems," I heard Stephen say to himself.

"Stephen, you have made your first mistake."

"What did I do?" he cried out dejectedly, already full of fear.

"You stopped."

"What do I do now? I feel like my feet are too heavy to move."

"Look at the hole you made in the fences," I said. "Now look at the top of that wall, and start walking. When you get to the wall, keep going. Do not stop to rest. There is no rest to be found by hanging on the side of that wall, so just keep climbing until you get to the top."

To my great relief, he started moving forward again. He was going much slower, but he was moving. When he got to the wall, he began to climb, slowly but steadily. When I knew that he was going to make it, I went to the wall and quickly climbed it so that I could meet him on the other side.

I knew Stephen would be thirsty, so I waited for him by a stream. When he got there, he was a little surprised to see me, but very glad. I was just as surprised to see the change in him. Not only were his eyes shining more brightly and clearly than ever, but he walked with a confidence and nobility that was stunning. I had seen him as a soldier of the cross, but I had not seen him as the great prince who he obviously was called to be.

"Tell me about it," I said.

"It was so hard to start walking again and then to keep walking, I knew that if I ever stopped, it might be too hard to ever start again. I thought about the ones you told me of, the ones who knew the name of the Lord, but had never climbed that wall to walk in faith in His name. I knew that I could become one of them. I decided that even if I fell, even if I died, I would rather die than stay in that prison. I would rather die than not see what is on this side and not make the journey that I am called to make. It was hard, even harder than I thought, but it is already worth it."

"Here, drink from this stream. You will find all of the water and food that you need on the journey. It will always be there when you really need it. Let the hunger and thirst keep you moving. When you find the refreshments, rest for as long as they last, and then keep going."

He drank quickly and then stood up, anxious to move on.

"I will not see you again for a time, so there are a few things that I must tell you now that will help you on the journey."

Stephen looked at me with a focus and brightness that was marvelous. Those who have known the greatest bondage will love liberty the most, I thought. I directed him to look at the highest mountain that we could see.

"You must now climb that mountain. When you get to the top, look for as far as you can see. Mark well what you see, and look for the path that will lead you to where you are going. Make a map of the way in your mind. That is where you are called to go."

"I understand," he replied. "But can it be seen from one of these lower mountains? I'm no longer afraid of climbing, but I am anxious to get on with the journey."

"You can see places from these lower mountains and get to those places much faster. You could choose to do that. It will take longer and be much harder to climb that high mountain, but from there you will be able to see much farther and see something much greater. The journey from the high mountain will also be more difficult and take longer. You are free, and you can choose either journey."

"You always take the highest mountain, don't you?" Stephen asked.

"I know now that it is always the best, but I cannot say that I have always chosen the highest mountain. I have often chosen the easiest, quickest way, and I was always sorry when I did. I now believe that it is wisdom to always choose the highest mountain to climb. I know that the greatest treasure is always at the end of the longest, most difficult journey. I think that you, too, are that kind of treasure hunter. You have overcome great fear. Now is the time to walk in great faith."

"I know that what you are saying is true, and I know in my heart that I must climb the highest mountain now or I will always choose that which is less than I could have had. I am just so anxious to get going and arrive at my destination."

"Faith and patience go together," I responded. "Impatience is really a lack of faith. Impatience will never lead you to the highest purposes of God. Good can be the greatest enemy of best. Now is the time to establish a pattern in your life of always choosing the highest and best. This is the way to remain close to Wisdom."

"What else are you supposed to tell me before I go?" Stephen asked, sitting on a rock, wisely choosing to be patient and receive all that he needed to know before he left. I thought that he might already know Wisdom better than I knew Him.

A Warning

"There is another wisdom that is not the wisdom of God, and there is another one who calls himself 'Wisdom.' He is *not* Wisdom; he is our enemy. He can be difficult to recognize because he tries to appear as Wisdom, and he is very good at it. He comes as an angel of light, and he usually brings truth. He will have a form of truth, and he has wisdom, but it has taken me a long time to be able to distinguish them from *the* Truth and *the* Wisdom. I have learned that I can still be fooled by him if for one moment I start to think that I can't. Wisdom has told me that we can never outsmart the enemy—our defense is to learn to first recognize, and then resist him."

Stephen's eyes were wide as that "knowing" look came over him. "I know who you are talking about!" he interjected.

"I met a lot of people in the prison who followed that one. They were always talking about a higher wisdom, a higher knowledge. They always seemed like noble, fair people, but they felt foul. Whenever I told them about Wisdom, they said that they knew 'Wisdom,' too, and that he was their 'inner guide.' However, when I listened to them, I did not feel I was being led to freedom like they said, but rather to an even stronger bondage in that prison. I just felt darkness around them, not like the light I felt when I talked with Wisdom. I knew they were not the same."

"The true Wisdom is Jesus. You know that now. True wisdom is to seek Him. Any wisdom that does not lead you to Jesus is a false wisdom. Jesus will always set you free. The false 'Wisdom' will always lead you to bondage. However, true freedom often looks like bondage at first, and bondage usually looks like freedom at first."

"It's not going to be easy is it?" Stephen lamented.

"No. It is not going to be easy, and it is not supposed to be. Suspicion is not the same as true discernment, but if you are going to suspect anything, suspect what seems easy. I have not yet found 'easy' through any door or on any path that has been right. Taking the easy way may be the surest way to be misled. You have been called as a soldier, and you are going to have to fight. Right now the whole world is in the power of the false 'Wisdom,' and you will have to overcome the world to fulfill your destiny."

"Already I have had to do things that were harder than anything I have ever done before," Stephen reflected. "But you are right—it is hard, but it is worth it. I have never known such joy, such satisfaction, such hope. Freedom is hard. It is hard to have to choose which mountain I climb. Back there, I knew that I could have chosen to not climb that wall. I felt like the fear of making that choice was the wall inside of me. But once I had made the choice, I knew I would make it over the top. But does it ever become easier?"

"I don't think so, but somehow 'hard' gets to be more fulfilling. There can be no victory without a battle, and the greater the battle, the greater the victory. The more victories you experience, the more you start to look forward to the battles, and you rise even higher to face the bigger ones. What makes it easy is that the Lord always leads us to victory. If you stay close to Him, you will never fail. After every battle, every test, you are much closer to Him and know Him much better."

"Will I always feel that darkness when the false 'Wisdom' tries to mislead me?"

"I don't know. I do know that the darkness comes when he deceives us into self-seeking. When he deceived the first man and woman into eating from the Tree of the Knowledge of Good and Evil, the first thing they did was to look at themselves. Once the false 'Wisdom' can make us self-centered, our fall into bondage is sure. The deceiver always tries to get you to seek yourself. The call to fulfill our destiny is not for our sake, but for the Lord's sake and for the sake of His people."

"Has anyone ever made it to their destiny without being tricked?"

"I don't think so. Even the great Apostle Paul admitted to having been foiled by Satan. Peter was tricked a few times that were recorded in Scripture, and we do not know how many other times that were not recorded. But don't be overly concerned about being deceived. That is actually one of his biggest traps. He sidetracks many by having them fear more in his power to deceive than to have faith in the power of the Holy Spirit to lead them into all truth. Those who have fallen into this trap not only fall into increasing bondage to fear, but they will attack anyone who walks in the freedom that comes with faith. I am quite sure that you will not make it far up that mountain before they ambush you."

"And they know the name of Jesus?" Stephen asked, a little confused. "They must have known His name to get over that wall and to have gone that far. I mean, didn't they really know His name once?"

"I am sure they did. But stand and look throughout the valley ahead around every mountain. What do you see?"

"It looks like little prisons. It looks like there are many just like the one I came out of!"

"That's why I was surprised when you told me that Wisdom had said this was the only prison, but after I was there for just a little while I understood what He meant. Look at the high walls. Look at the fences. They are all the same. If you are captured along the way, they will not bring you back here. They know you would choose death over that, but they will take you to one of the other prisons. When you get close to them, it is hard to see that they are prisons from the outside, but inside they are all the same, with people divided and imprisoned by their fears."

"I'm glad you showed them to me," Stephen offered. "I did not even see the prisons when I was looking this way from the top of the wall or when I was looking for the mountain I am to climb. And you think I will be ambushed many times by those who will try to capture me and put me in one of them? And these people will be using the name of Jesus?"

"The Lord, Himself, warns in Scripture that in the last days many will come in His name, claiming that He is indeed the Christ, and yet they will deceive many. Believe me, there are many like that, and I do not believe that most of them know they are deceivers. I can tell you a characteristic I have seen in all those whom I have met—they quit while on their journey, stopping short of their destiny. It takes faith to keep going, and they choose to follow fear rather than faith. They begin to think that fear is faith and actually see the walls of fear around their prisons as strongholds of truth. Fear will do that to your vision, and you can start to see strongholds that way. Few of these people are really dishonest. They are sincere, but they are deceived by one of the most powerful deceptions of all, *the fear of deception.*"

"Should I fight them?"

"I understand your question and have asked it many times myself. They destroy the faith of so many and do far more damage to the sojourners than all of the cults and sects combined. There will be a time when all such stumbling blocks will be removed, but for now they, too, are serving a purpose by making the way harder."

"Wisdom wants it to be harder? It is already so difficult just battling our own fears. Why does He want to make it harder by making us battle all of these fearful people as well?"

"The journey will be exactly as easy or hard as He wants it to be. This life is a temporary journey used to prepare those who will reign with Him over the age to come as sons and daughters of the Most High forever. Every trial is for the purpose of changing us into His image. One of the first things we must learn on this journey is not to waste a single trial, but to seize them as the opportunities that they are. If your path is more difficult, it is because of your high calling."

The Necessity of Discipline

"Many are called, but few are chosen. Many will come to the wedding feast, but few will be the bride."

We turned to see Wisdom standing behind us. He appeared as the young athlete that Stephen had come to know.

"Run the race that is set before you, and the prize will be greater than you can understand at this time. You know the discipline that it takes to prepare for the race. Now discipline yourself for righteousness. I have called all to run, but few run so as to win. Discipline yourself to win."

Then He was gone.

"Why did He leave?" Stephen asked.

"He said all that needed to be said at this time. He spoke to you of discipline. I would take that to be a most important word for you at this time."

"Discipline. I used to hate that word!"

"He spoke to you about the race. Were you a runner?"

"Yes, I am very fast. I was always the fastest one in my school and was even offered a scholarship to run for a major university."

"I take it that you did not accept it."

"No, I didn't."

"Was it because of a lack of discipline that you did not go to college?"

"No! It was..." There was a long silence as Stephen looked down at his feet. "Yes, I think it probably was."

"Don't worry about that now. However, you must understand something. Most who are potentially the best in every field or occupation never even become high achievers for the lack of that one thing—discipline. What you are doing now is much more important than track or college. Obviously discipline has been a weakness of yours, and it has cost you much already, but in Christ all things become new. In Him, the very things that have been your greatest weaknesses can become your greatest strengths. You are now His disciple. That means that you are 'a disciplined one.'"

"I know that you are telling me the truth, and I know that this is one race I do not want to lose."

"Do you see the path leading up the mountain?"

"Yes."

"Its name is Discipline. Stay on it if you want to reach the top."

CHAPTER X

the army

Suddenly, I was standing on a high mountain overlooking a great plain. Before me, there was an army marching on a wide front. There were 12 divisions in the vanguard that stood out sharply from the great multitude of soldiers who followed behind them. These divisions were further divided into what I assumed to be regiments, battalions, companies and squads. The divisions were distinguished by their banners, and the regiments were distinguished by their different colored uniforms.

Battalions, companies and squads were distinguished by such things as sashes or epaulets that each different group wore. All wore armor that was polished silver, shields that appeared to be pure gold, and weapons that were both silver and gold. The banners were huge, 30 to 40 feet long. As the soldiers marched, their armor and weapons flashed in the sun like lightning, and the flapping of the banners and the tread of their feet sounded like rolling thunder. I did not think that the earth had ever witnessed anything like this before.

Then I was close enough to see their faces—male and female, old and young from every race. There was a fierce resolution on their faces, yet they did not seem tense. War was in the air, but in the ranks I could sense such a profound peace that I knew that not a single one feared the battle to which they were marching. The spiritual atmosphere that I felt when close to them was as awesome as their appearance.

I looked at their uniforms. The colors were brilliant. Every soldier also wore rank insignias and medals. The generals and other higher ranking officers marched in the ranks with the others. Although it was obvious that those with higher rank were in charge, no one seemed overly sensitive to their rank. From the highest ranking officer to the lowest, they all seemed to be close friends. It was an army of what seemed to be unprecedented discipline, yet it also seemed to be just one big family.

As I studied them, they seemed selfless—not because they lacked identity, but because they were all so sure of who they were and what they were doing. They were not consumed with themselves or seeking recognition. I could not detect ambition or pride anywhere in the ranks. It was stunning to see so many who were so unique, yet in such harmony and marching in perfect step. I was sure that there had never been an army on earth like this.

Then I was behind the front divisions looking at a much larger group that was composed of hundreds of divisions. Each of these was a different size, with the smallest numbering about two thousand and the largest in the hundreds of thousands. Although this group was not as sharp and colorful as the first one, this also was an awesome army simply because of its size. This group also had banners, but they were not nearly as large and impressive as those of the first group's. They all had uniforms and ranks, but I was surprised that many of these did not even have on a full set of armor, and many did not have weapons. The armor and weapons that they did have were not nearly as polished and bright as those of the first group.

As I looked more closely at those in these ranks, I could see that they were all determined and had purpose, but they did not have nearly the focus of the first group. These seemed much more aware of their own rank and the rank of those around them. I felt that this was a distraction hindering their focus. I could also sense ambition and jealousy in the ranks, which unquestionably was a further distraction. Even so, I felt that this second division still had a higher level of devotion and purpose than any army on earth. This, too, was a very powerful force.

Behind this second army, there was a third one which marched so far behind the first two armies that I was not sure they could even see the groups ahead of them. This group was many times larger than the first and second armies combined, seemingly composed of millions and millions. As I watched from a distance, this army would move in different directions like a great flock of birds, sweeping first one way and then the next, never moving in a straight direction for very long. Because of this erratic movement, it was drifting farther and farther from the first two groups.

As I came closer, I saw that these soldiers had on tattered, dull gray uniforms which were neither pressed nor clean. Almost everyone was bloody and wounded. A few were attempting to march, but most just walked in the general direction in which the others were headed. Fights were constantly breaking out in the ranks causing many of the wounds. Some of the soldiers were trying to stay close to the frayed banners scattered throughout their ranks. Even so, not even those near the banners had a clear identity because they were constantly drifting from one banner to another.

In this third army, I was surprised that there were only two ranks—generals and privates. Only a few had a piece of armor on, and I did not see any weapons except dummy weapons which were carried by the generals. The generals flaunted these dummy weapons as if having them made the officers special, but even those in the ranks could tell that the weapons were not real. This was sad because it was obvious that those in the ranks desperately wanted to find someone who was real whom they could follow.

There did not seem to be any ambition except among the generals. This was not because of selflessness as in the first army, but because there was so little caring. I thought that at least the ambition present in the second group would be much better than the confusion that prevailed in this group. The generals here seemed to be more intent on talking about themselves and fighting with one another, which the little groups around the banners were constantly doing. I could then see that the battles within the ranks were the cause of the great sweeping, erratic changes of directions that this group would make from time to time.

As I looked at the millions in the last group, I felt that even with their great numbers, they did not actually add strength to the army, but rather weakened it. In a real battle, they would be much more of a liability than an asset. Just sustaining them with food and protection would cost more in resources than any value they could add to the army's ability to fight. I thought that a private in the first or second group would be worth more than many generals from the third. I could not understand why the first groups even allowed this group to tag along behind them. They obviously were not true soldiers.

The Wisdom of Zipporah

I was suddenly on a mountain where I could see the entire army. As I watched, I noticed that the plain was dry and dusty before the army, but immediately after the first twelve divisions passed, the earth was dark green, with trees giving shade and bearing fruit and pure streams flowing throughout the land. This army was restoring the earth. I thought of how different this was from what would happen when one of the world's armies would pass through a land. They would plunder and forage until the land was utterly stripped wherever they had marched.

I watched as the second divisions passed over the same ground. They left bridges and many buildings, but the ground was not left in as good a shape as before they had passed. The grass was not as green, the streams were somewhat muddied, and much of the fruit had been taken.

Then I saw what happened as the third group passed over the same ground. The grass was either gone or so trampled into the earth that it could not be seen. The few trees that remained were stripped. The streams were polluted. The bridges were broken down and impassable. The buildings were left in shambles. It seemed that this group had undone all of the good that the first two had done. As I watched them, anger welled up inside of me.

I felt Wisdom standing beside me. He did not say anything for a long time, but I could sense that He also was angry.

"Selfishness destroys," He finally said. *"I came to give life and to give it abundantly. Even when My army has matured, there will be many who call on My name and follow those who follow Me, but they do not know Me or walk in My ways. These destroy the fruit of those who follow Me. Because of this, the world does not know whether to consider My people a blessing or a curse."*

As Wisdom said this, I felt immense heat coming from Him, intensifying until it was so painful that it was hard for me to concentrate on what He was saying. Even so, I knew that I was feeling what He was feeling and that it was an important part of the message which He was conveying to me. The pain was a combination of compassion for the earth and anger at the selfishness in this army. Both feelings were so strong that I felt as though they were being branded into me.

As the anger of the Lord continued to rise, I felt that He might destroy the entire army. Then I remembered how the Lord had met Moses when he was on his way to Egypt in obedience to the Lord. The Lord sought to put him to death until his wife, Zipporah, circumcised their son. I had never understood this until now. Because circumcision speaks of the removal of the fleshly, or carnal nature, the incident with

Moses was like a prophetic foreshadowing of the sin of Eli, the priest, who had brought a curse upon himself and defeat to Israel because he had failed to discipline his sons.

"Lord, raise up those with the wisdom of Zipporah!" I cried out.

The burning continued and a deep determination came over me to go to the leaders of this great army and tell them the story of Zipporah and that everyone in the Lord's army had to be circumcised in their hearts. The carnal nature had to be cut away. I knew that if they marched any farther before this was done, the entire army was in danger of being destroyed by the Lord Himself, just as He had almost killed Moses when he was returning to Egypt.

Then I was standing in the Hall of Judgment before the Judgment Seat. The Lord still appeared as Wisdom, but I had never seen Him more fierce, nor His words come with more weight.

"You have already seen this army in your heart many times. The leaders I am commissioning now will lead this army. I am sending you to many of these leaders. What will you say to them?"

"Lord, this is a great army, but I am still grieved about the condition of the third group. I do not understand why they are even allowed to pretend to be a part of Your army. I would like to say that before they went any farther, the first and second armies should turn and drive away this third group. They were really very little more than a huge mob."

"What you saw today is still in the future. The ministries I am about to release will gather this army and equip them to be all that you saw. At this time, almost My entire army is in the condition of the third group. How can I let them be driven away?"

I was stunned by this, although I knew that I had never seen any of the Lord's people who were in as good shape as even the second group of this army.

"Lord, I know I felt Your anger at this group. If almost Your entire army is now in that condition, I am just thankful that You have not destroyed all of us. When I was looking at this third group, I felt that their deplorable condition was due to a lack of training, equipping and vision, as well as a failure to embrace the cross that circumcises the heart. I believe I must go to them with the message about Zipporah, but they also need drill sergeants and officers who will train them."

Wisdom continued, *"Remember the first army that you saw before the mountain. They, too, were unprepared for the battle, and when the battle began, those who were not prepared fled. However, many returned with their armor on and their delusions replaced with truth. The first two groups in this army were also changed by battles that woke them up to their true condition. Then they cried out to Me and I sent them shepherds after My own heart.*

"All of My shepherds are like King David. They are not hirelings who seek their own place or position, but they will lay down their lives for My people. They are also fearless in warfare against My enemies and pure in their worship of Me. I am about to send these shepherds forth. You must return with the message of Zipporah. The time is coming soon when I will not abide those who seek to be counted with My people but do not circumcise their hearts. You must warn them of My wrath.

"I am also sending you back to walk with the prophets I am sending forth as Samuels to pour oil upon My true shepherds. Many of these are now considered the least of their brethren, but you will find them serving as faithful shepherds of their little flocks, faithful laborers in whatever I have given them to do. These are My faithful ones who are called to be kings. These I will trust with My authority. They will prepare My people for the great battle at the end."

I then wondered in my heart, If we are now in the condition of the third group, what was to be done with the generals who did not seem to be real generals at all?

"You are right, they are not real generals," the Lord answered. *"I did not appoint them, but they appointed themselves. Even so, some of them will be changed and I will make them generals. Others will become useful officers. However, most will flee at the first sight of battle, and you will not see them again.*

"Remember this: At one time everyone in the first two groups was a part of the last one. When you go with the message of Zipporah

declaring that I will no longer tolerate the carnality of My people, those whom I have truly called and are devoted to obeying Me will not run from My circumcision but will stand against the carnality in the camp so that I will not have to bring judgment upon them. My shepherds are responsible for the condition of My sheep. My generals are responsible for the condition of My soldiers. Those whom I have called will take this responsibility because they love Me, they love My people, and they love righteousness."

Captain of the Host

Then I was no longer before the Judgment Seat, but on the mountain overlooking the army again. Wisdom was standing beside me. He was resolute, but I no longer felt the pain and anger that I did before.

"I have allowed you see a little into the future," Wisdom began. *"I am sending you to those who are called to prepare My army and lead it. These are the ones who have been fighting the battle on the mountain. These are the ones who have met the army of the accuser and remained faithful. These are the ones who have watched over My people and protected them at the risk of their own lives. They are called to be leaders in My army who will fight in the great battle at the end and will stand without fear against all of the powers of darkness.*

"As you can see, this army is marching, but there will be times when it camps. The camping is as important as the marching. It is

the time for planning, training and sharpening skills and weapons. It is also time for those in the first group to walk among the second and for the leaders of the second group to walk among the third group, finding those who can be called to the next level. Do this while you can, for the time is near when Revelation 11:1-2 will be fulfilled, and those who want to be called by My name but do not walk in My ways will be trodden underfoot. Before the last great battle, My army will be holy, even as I am holy. I will remove those who are not circumcised of heart and the leaders who do not uphold My righteousness. When the last battle is fought, there will be no third group as you see here.

"Until now when My army has camped, most of the time has been wasted. Just as I only lead My people forward with a clear objective, so it is that when I call My army to camp, there is a purpose. The strength of the army that marches will be determined by the quality of its camp. When it is time to stop and camp for a season, it is to teach My people My ways. An army is an army whether it is in battle or at peace. You must learn how to camp, how to march, and how to fight. You will not do any one of these well unless you do them all well.

"My army must be ready to do each of these in season and out of season. You may think that it is time to march, but I will direct you to camp because I see things that you can never see, even from this place of vision. If you follow me, you will always be doing the

right thing at the right time, even though it may not seem right to you. Remember, I am the Captain of the Host.

"An army's resolve will be determined by the nobility of their mission, how well they are prepared for their mission, and how well they are led. This army will march with the most noble mission that has ever been given to man. However, few of My people are being equipped for their mission, and those who are now leading My people follow their own desires. I will now raise up leaders who will train and equip My people. These will always follow Me because I am the Captain of the Host.

"Many armies experience both victories and defeats. My army has been marching for many centuries. It, too, has had many victories and many defeats. My army has lost many battles because it attacked the enemy when I did not give the command. Others were defeated because they attacked the enemy with untrained people. Most of these leaders have done this because they were seeking their own glory. As Paul wrote of those in his own time, 'They all seek after their own interests.'

"Other leaders have had My interests at heart and sincerely sought a victory over evil for My name's sake, but they did not train their people well; they did not walk with Me as their Wisdom. That will now change. I will be the Captain of the Host. Do not be discouraged by the way My people now appear, but remember what they will become. I will now raise up leaders who will only march when I give the orders. When My army follows Me, it will win every *battle. When they camp, they will know My presence, and they will grow strong in My ways.*

"You will come to a time in the future when you see My army exactly as it is now. At that time, you will feel My burning anger. Know that I will no longer abide those who remain in the condition of the third group. Then I will stop the march of the entire army until those in this group have been disciplined to become soldiers or dispersed. I will discipline those in the second group to cast off their evil ambitions and live for Me and My Truth. Then My army will march forth, not to destroy, but to give life. I will be in the midst of them to tread My enemies under this army's feet. I am coming to be the Captain of the Host!"

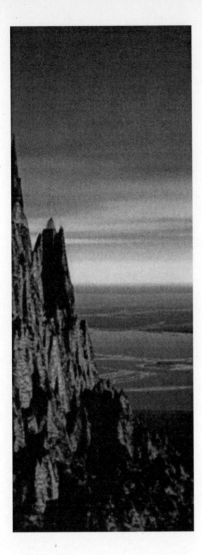

CHAPTER XI

the city

I then stood upon another mountain looking out over a city. The glory of this city was beyond anything I had seen or imagined before. While every building and home was unique and beautiful, each fit into a breathtaking, overall symmetry with one another and the surrounding fields, mountains and bodies of water. It was almost as if the city grew like a plant instead of being built. I felt that I was looking at something that had been built by a race that had not fallen and had walked in the righteousness and purity of Adam and Eve in the beginning.

One feature that stood out was the large amount of glass windows in each structure or dwelling. This glass was so clear and clean, and the windows and doors were so situated that I sensed that I was not only welcome in each dwelling, but invited. It was also as if nothing was hidden, and there was no danger of anything being stolen.

Then I looked at the people in the city. They seemed familiar, but at the same time I knew that I had never met anyone like them. They were like I imagined Adam to be before the fall. The eyes of each one shone with what seemed to be almost total comprehension, an intellectual depth far beyond even the most brilliant person I had ever known. I knew this to be the result of an order and peace that was completely free of confusion or doubt, or maybe the confusion *of* doubt. There was no ambition because each one was so confident and had so much joy in who they were and what they were doing. Because everyone here was free, they were also completely open. Poverty or sickness seemed incomprehensible.

I looked at the streets in this city. There were many major highways in the center all going in the same direction, and many smaller roads connected these great highways. As I looked at one of the largest of the highways, knowledge was imparted to me about the truth of holiness. I looked at another highway and knew the truth about healing. As I looked at another, I began to understand things about judgment. Looking at each street, I understood a different truth. I then realized that each highway was a path to that truth. The people walking and living on each one seemed to reflect the truth of that highway.

My attention turned to the many streets connecting the highways. As I looked at each of these, I felt an impartation

154

of a fruit of the Spirit, such as love, joy, peace or patience. These came as feelings instead of the understanding that came when I looked at the highways.

I noticed that while some of these streets were connected to every highway, some of the highways only had one or two streets connected to them. For example, I could only get to the Highway of Holiness by walking on the street of Love. I could only get to the Highway of Judgment by walking on the streets of Love or Joy. However, the Highway of Grace was joined by *all* of the streets. To get on any of the Highways of Truth, I had to walk on a street named after a fruit of the Spirit.

People were walking on the highways and streets, while some were sitting on the edges of them. Some were in the houses on a street or highway, and others were building houses on them. Those living in the houses were constantly serving food and drink to those who were walking or sitting. I then noticed that there were no restaurants, hotels or hospitals in the city. I quickly understood that none of these were needed because every home was a center of hospitality and healing.

Almost every home was open to the travelers. Those that were not open were used for special purposes, such as study or long-term healing. I wondered why anyone would even need healing here, but later I would be shown the reason. Even so, I could not imagine a more wonderful place for

155

this great ministry of hospitality, helps or healing, even those being built on the Highway of Judgment, which seemed to be the place of the most activity. Because of this, even the Highway of Judgment was appealing. It was apparent that every street was not only safe, but was more desirable than any other road or highway I had ever seen, even in theme parks. This city was far more glorious than any utopia of which philosophers could conceive.

My attention was drawn back to the Highway of Judgment. It seemed to have been the least traveled highway, but now was becoming much more active. I then saw that this was because the other streets and highways all flowed toward this one. However, even though the Highway of Judgment was becoming the center of activity, people still seemed hesitant to enter it.

As I looked toward the end of the highway, I could see that the road was on a steady incline, and there was a high mountain at the end which was enveloped in a subtle, but profound, glory. I knew that if people could see the end of this road, there would have been far more traveling on it. I then realized that I was drawn to this road because it had the same feeling to it as the Great Hall of Judgment. I knew that this was the road that led to knowing the Lord as the Righteous Judge.

The Bond of Peace

I wondered if this city was heaven or the New Jerusalem. Then I observed that even though these people were of stature far beyond any I had seen on earth, they did not have the glory or stature of those in even the lowest positions in the Hall of Judgment. I was wondering about this when I felt Wisdom standing next to me again.

"These are the same people who you saw in My army," He began. *"The city and the army are the same. My coming leaders have had visions of both My army and My city. I am building both, and I will use the leaders I am now preparing to complete what I began generations ago. My generals will become master-builders for My city, and My master builders will also become generals. These are the same.*

"One day, the army will no longer be needed, but this city will last forever. You must prepare the army for its present battles, but build all that you build for the future.

"There is a future for the earth. After My judgments have come, it will be a glorious future. I am about to show My people the future so that the future will be in their hearts. As Solomon wrote, 'Everything God does will remain forever.' As My people become like Me, they will build that which will last. They will do all that they do with a peace for the present times and a vision for the future. The city that I am building to last forever is built on truth in the

hearts of men. My truth will endure, and those who walk in truth will leave fruit that will remain.

"I am coming to earth in My people as Wisdom to build My city. The knowledge of truth will fill My city, but wisdom will build it. The wisdom that is coming upon My builders will cause the world to marvel at My city even more than it marveled at the city that Solomon built. Men have worshiped their own wisdom since they first ate of the Tree of Knowledge. The world's wisdom is about to pale before My wisdom which I will reveal through My city. Then those who worship any other wisdom will be ashamed. All that Solomon did was a prophecy of what I am about to build.

"In all that you have seen of the city that I am building, I have only given you a superficial glimpse. From time to time, you will be shown more, but for now you must see one thing. What did you notice the most about this city?"

"The one thing that stood out the most to me was the harmony. Everything in the city fit so perfectly together, and the whole city fit so perfectly in its environment," I responded.

"The perfect bond of peace is love," the Lord continued. *"In My city, there will be unity. In all that I created, there was harmony. All things fit together in Me. Everything that I am doing in the earth is to restore the original harmony between My Father and His creation and among all creatures. When mankind lives in harmony with Me, the earth will be in harmony with Him, and there will*

be no more earthquakes, floods or storms. I came to bring peace on earth."

As He spoke, I knew I was looking into the future, just as I had looked when I viewed the army. I also knew that what He had said about building with peace in the present and a vision for the future was also essential for the harmony I saw. Time was also a part of His creation within which we had to fit.

Wisdom then turned me so that I looked directly into His eyes and said, *"I love My creation. I love the beasts of the field and the fish of the sea. I will restore all things as they were intended to be, but I must first restore mankind. I did not come just to redeem, but to restore. To be a part of My ministry of restoration you must not just see others as they are, but as they are to become. Like Ezekiel, you must see in even the driest bones an exceedingly great army. You must prophesy life to the bones until they become the army that I have called them to be. Then My army will march. When My army marches, it will restore—not destroy. It will fight evil, but it will also build the city of righteousness.*

"All of the treasures of the earth cannot weigh in the balance with the value of a single soul. I am building My city in the hearts of men, with the hearts of men. Those who keep the great wisdom— the knowledge of the eternal treasures—will be used to build My city. You will know My builders by this wisdom—they do not set their minds on earthly things, but on the treasures of heaven. Because

of this, the world will bring its wealth to My city just as they did in the times of Solomon.

"I am about to release My wise master builders. You must walk with them, and they must all walk together. Each of the highways and streets that you saw in this city will begin as a fortress of truth in the earth. Each fortress will stand against the powers of darkness, and those powers will not be able to stand against them. Each will be like a mountain, with rivers flowing from it to water the earth. Each will be a city of refuge and a haven for all who seek Me. No weapon that is formed against them will prosper, and no weapon that I give to them will fail."

The Lord's Builders

As Wisdom spoke, my eyes were opened to see the most beautiful valley I had ever seen. The mountains forming the valley and the valley, itself, were more green than any green I could remember having seen. The rocks were like fortresses made of silver; the trees were perfect and full. There was a river in the middle fed by streams flowing from every mountain around it. The water sparkled with a blue that was the bluest tint I had ever seen and beautifully matched the sky. Every blade of grass was perfect. The valley was filled with many kinds of animals which all seemed to be the very best of their breed with no diseases or scars. They fit perfectly with the valley and with one another. I had never seen such a desirable place on earth.

I wondered if I was seeing the Garden of Eden, and then I saw a few soldiers in full armor who were surveying the valley. Other soldiers were following each stream to the river, and then following the river to the place where the first soldiers were surveying. At first I did not think that the soldiers fit in this place at all, but for some reason I was quickly at ease with them because I somehow knew they were supposed to be there.

I looked at the soldiers. They were rough and battle-hardened, yet kind and approachable. They were fierce and resolute, yet seemed to be at perfect peace. They were serious and sober, yet full of joy and quick to laugh. I thought that even though war is always terrible, if I had to go to battle, there was no other group of soldiers beside whom I would rather fight.

I noticed their armor which seemed to have been custom made just for them, fitting so perfectly that they moved with a grace as though they were not wearing any armor at all. I could tell that it was both lighter, yet stronger than any I had ever seen. The armor also seemed to be a perfect combination of the colors of the water, mountains and blue sky, which I soon realized was the reflection of these colors in a purity I had never before seen in a reflection. The armor itself was of an "other-worldly" silver, deeper and purer than any silver on earth. As I was wondering who these soldiers were, the Lord began to speak.

"In My Father's house are many dwelling places," He replied. *"These are My builders. Each of My houses will be a fortress from which I will send out My armies. Some will go forth as knights to fight for the poor and oppressed, while others will go forth as small companies who will raid the strongholds of the enemy and bring back the spoils. Some will send forth a host to conquer cities over which My truth and righteousness will reign, and others will join with armies from other fortresses to liberate whole nations with My truth, My love and My power.*

"These fortresses are not just for the protection of My people, but for mobilizing, training and sending forth My army throughout the earth. The darkest of times will soon come, but My people will not be found hiding. They will go forth to conquer evil with good. They will conquer by not loving their lives even unto death and by loving others more than their own lives. These will be the fearless ones whom I will send forth before I return.

"Even the prophecies of their coming strike terror into the hearts of My enemies. They will have no fear. They will love. Love is more powerful than fear, and their love will break the power of fear that has held mankind in bondage since the beginning. Because they have chosen to die daily, the fear of death has no power over them. This will give them power over every enemy whose power is fear. I was once dead, but now am alive forever, and those who know Me

cannot fear death. Therefore, those who know Me will follow Me wherever I go.

"Each of My dwelling places will be in a valley like this. It is alive with the life that was in the earth before the fall because here the power of My redemption has brought forth true life again. My dwelling places will only be found where all of My streams flow together into one. My builders will come from every stream, but they will work as one. Just as great houses need different craftsmen, so does My house. Only when they work together can they build My house.

"As you see in these, My builders will have the wisdom to complete the survey before they build. Each of My houses will fit perfectly into the land where they are located, not according to human measurements, but according to Mine. The first skill that My builders develop is the skill of surveying. They must know the land because I designed the land for My people. When you build with My wisdom, what you build will fit perfectly with the land."

Then I was standing by one of the streams in the valley. I started following it to the top of a mountain. As I got close to the top, I began to hear loud, terrible sounds. When I looked beyond the valley, I could see wars and great earthquakes tearing the earth, and storms and fires that seemed to completely encircle the valley. It was as if I was standing on the border between heaven and hell, looking into hell itself. I somehow knew that all of hell was powerless to encroach on the valley, but the sight was so terrible, I turned to run back into the valley. I then felt Wisdom standing beside me.

"This is where you must live, between the dying and the living. Do not fear, but believe. You have been weak, but now I am with you, so be courageous and strong. Fear must not rule over you—do nothing because of fear. Do what you do because of love, and you will always triumph. Love is the source of courage. Love will prevail in the end. Encourage My builders with these words."

CHAPTER XII

WORDS OF LIFE

Then I was back at the Great Hall of Judgment, standing before the same door again. I was still a little stunned by what I had seen on the edge of the valley, but His words were still resounding in me. "Love, love," I repeated over and over. "I must not forget the power of love. There is perfect peace in love. There is courage in love. There is power in love."

I looked at the door. I knew that this was the door to His church. I knew that the fortresses that Wisdom talked about were churches and movements. I began to think of some congregations and movements which I knew were already preparing for what I had seen. I began thinking of spiritual surveyors whom I knew but had never thought of in this way before. Then again, it seemed like most of them were so battle-weary that they were just trying to survive, even fighting one another in their desperation.

167

I thought of the battle that had been fought on the mountain. The enemy had used Christians to attack other Christians who were trying to climb the mountain. Even though that battle was eventually won and most of the Christians freed from the accuser's power, I knew that it would take a long time for the wounds from those battles to heal. Many had been under the influence of the accuser for so long that it was still a part of their nature to accuse, and it could be a while before their minds were renewed. I knew that the church was still a very long way from being united.

Where do we begin? I thought to myself. What can I do if I go through that door?

"You do not have to begin. It is already finished," Wisdom answered. *"I accomplished the unity of My people on the cross. Even though it looks like the enemy has prevailed since the cross, he actually only has worked into the plan which My Father and I had from the beginning. When you preach the cross and live by its power, you will do My will. Those who serve Me and not their own ambitions will soon recognize one another and be joined together. Those who have the true fear of God do not have to fear anything on the earth. Those who fear Me will not fear one another, but will love each other and sit together at My table.*

"I have called you to see, and you will see how My kingdom will come. The devil will be cast down to the earth and will come to the earth with great wrath. But do not fear his wrath, for I am also about to show My wrath against all iniquity. The evil one and

all who follow evil will soon know My wrath. You must see these things, but you are not to fear them because I dwell in the midst of My people and am greater than all. As you behold Me you will not fear. If you fear, it is because you are not beholding Me.

"When the evil in mankind has become fully united with the evil one, the great time of trouble will come upon the earth. Then all of mankind and the whole creation will understand the futility and tragedy of rebellion. At the same time, My people will become fully united with Me, and My great light will stand against the great darkness. Those who walk in lawlessness will fall into the deep darkness. Those who walk in obedience will shine forth as the stars of heaven.

"Humility and obedience will always lead to Me. As you come to Me, you will behold and manifest My glory. The heavens and the earth are about to behold the difference between the light and the darkness. You are called to live between the darkness and the light, in order to call those who live in darkness to the light. Even now I do not desire for any to perish."

In the glory that surrounded us, it was difficult to remember the darkness and terrible events that I had just witnessed. I thought of the difference between His glory and even the greatest pomp and splendor of man. "How pitifully insignificant we are!" I blurted out. "If all of mankind could just have a glimpse of Your Judgment Seat they would all quickly repent. Lord, why do You not just show Yourself to the world so it will not have to endure this evil? No one would choose evil if they could see You as You are."

"I will reveal Myself. When evil has run its full course, then I will show Myself to the world. As the evil one is being revealed through fallen men, I will be revealed through restored men. Then the world will see Me—not just the glory that I have in heaven, but as My glory stands against the darkness. My glory is more than what you see here; it is My nature. After I reveal My nature in My people, I will return in the glory that I have here. Until then, I am seeking those who will follow Me because they love Me and love the truth, not just because they love this glory and power.

"Those who choose to obey when the whole world is disobeying are worthy to be heirs with Me. These will be worthy to rule with Me, to see My glory, and to share it. These are the ones who do not live for themselves, but for Me. Some of the greatest of these brethren of mine are about to be revealed. They will stand for truth against the greatest darkness. They will remain steadfast through the greatest trials. I have brought you here, and I am sending you back to encourage them to stand and not faint for the time of their salvation is near.

"I am also sending you back to warn these mighty ones. Satan saw the glory of My Father and beheld the myriads who serve Him, yet he still fell. He fell because he started to trust in the glory and power that the Father had shared with him instead of trusting the Father. Those who will be entrusted with the power and glory I share with them in these times must not put their trust in the power

or glory, but in Me. True faith is never in yourself, your wisdom or the power that I have given to you. True faith is in Me.

"As you grow in the true faith that is in Me, you will grow in dependence on Me, and you will trust yourself less. Those who begin to trust in themselves will not be able to carry the weight of My power or glory; they can fall just as the evil one did. My strength is made perfect in weakness, but you must never forget that in yourself you are weak, and by yourself you are foolish.

"Those who are worthy to reign with Me in the age to come will prove this by living in the darkness and weakness of human flesh, yet they will serve and trust Me. Even the greatest angels will gladly bow before those who have been proven in this way. The angels marvel when suffering men and women who have beheld so little of the glory here remain steadfast for Me and My truth in times of darkness. These are worthy to be called My brethren and to be called the sons and daughters of My Father.

"On earth, the truth often looks weak and easily defeated. Those who see from here know that My truth always prevails. The time when I stand up and bring My judgments to the earth has only been delayed so that My brethren could prove their love for Me by standing for truth at any cost. My truth and My goodness will prevail for all of eternity, and so will all who come to Me because they love the truth. These will shine forth as the stars which were made in honor of them."

As Wisdom continued to speak, it was like being washed in a shower of living water. At times I had been ashamed because even in the presence of His glory, I was as dull and easily distracted here as I was on earth. But now as He spoke to me, His words cleansed me so that a sharpness came to my mind beyond just mental exhilaration. The more I was cleansed, the more His words seemed to explode with cleansing brilliance. I not only saw His glory, but *felt* His glory inside of me. In His presence, I did not just hear the truth, I *absorbed* the truth.

His Beloved Bride

This sensation of being cleansed by His words was more wonderful than can be described, but it was familiar. I knew that I had felt this when listening to anointed preaching from one who had been in the presence of the Lord. It was not intoxicating, but the exact opposite. Instead of dulling the senses, it quickened them. In His presence, I felt that thousands of fragments of information which I had accumulated over the years were all tied together to give a deep and comprehensive meaning to everything He said. In this way, every concept became like a strong pillar of knowledge in my mind. Then it became a passion as I felt a deep love for each truth.

When He spoke, there was an energy released that enabled me to see each truth with a greater depth than ever before. His words did not just impart information, but *life*. This great illumination was similar to what I experienced after I decided not to try and hide anything when I was standing in front of the Judgment Seat. The more I opened my heart to His words to expose any darkness in me and to change me, the more power His words seemed to have in me.

The Lord did not just give information when He spoke, but somehow rearranged my mind and heart so that these truths would be the foundation for understanding, and the understanding released a love for the truth. For example, I had what I thought was a sound understanding of the church as the bride of Christ. As He talked about the ministries being sent forth to prepare His bride, I saw in my heart what seemed to be every church I knew. They immediately became much more than just a group of people; they became *His Beloved*. I felt a burning passion to help them prepare for Him. The repulsion of sin and harlotry with the world almost buckled my knees as I saw what it did to His people. I knew that I was feeling what He was feeling.

His cleansing truth poured over me. The cleanness I felt was more wonderful than I had ever believed possible. It was almost as if I had been living my life in a sewer and was now being given a hot shower. The power of cleansing truth gripped me so powerfully that I desperately wanted to carry it back to share with His people.

"I am about to release the power of anointed truth to cleanse My people," Wisdom continued. *"My bride will be cleansed of all of her defilements. I am sending forth My messengers who will*

be flames of fire, burning with zeal for My holiness and the holiness of My people."

As He spoke, I felt the depth and power of the message of holiness. I then knew without question the power of truth to accomplish this. A vision of the glorious bride whom He so deserves was burned into my heart. I passionately wanted to share this with His people so that they would become completely focused on getting ready for Him. I just could not comprehend doing anything again without this being my purpose.

He began to speak about the fortresses of truth and righteousness. While He talked, I saw the congregations with whom I was familiar and how they were struggling. I became burdened as never before for them to be empowered with His truth. I knew that they were weak because they were not walking in truth. The grief that I felt for them became almost more than I could bear.

"Why do they not walk in truth?" I blurted out.

"You are beginning to feel the burden that Nehemiah felt when he heard that Jerusalem was in distress because her walls were broken down," Wisdom explained. *"I am imparting to My messengers the fire to see My bride cleansed, and I am also imparting to them the burden of Nehemiah to see the walls of salvation restored. Then My people will no longer be in distress.*

174

"You have seen My people as My army, My city and My bride. Now you do not just see these, but you feel them. Only when My truth comes from the heart does it have the power to change men. Living waters must come from the innermost being—the heart. Just as you felt My truth cleansing you, I am making My messengers flames of fire who will speak truth, not to just give understanding, but with the power to change men's hearts. The truth that I am sending will not just convict My people of their sin, but will cleanse them from their sin."

Even as He was speaking, a great zeal rose up within me to do something. Divine strategies began coming to me which I knew could help His people. I could not wait to begin. I now believed that even the driest bones were going to become an exceedingly great army! In the presence of Wisdom, nothing seemed impossible. I had no trouble believing that His church would become a bride without spot or wrinkle, or that His church would become a great city, standing as a fortress of truth for the whole world to behold. I had no doubt that His people, even as weak and defeated as they now seemed, were about to become an army of truth before which no power of darkness could stand. Feeling the power of truth as never before, I knew that His power was much greater than the darkness.

Words of Life

In His presence, I felt as if I could speak forth the vision I had received of His bride and whoever heard it be changed. It seemed that I could speak to the most defeated little congregation with such power that they would quickly become a mighty fortress of truth. I also knew that on earth, my words did not have that power.

"Your words will have this power when you abide in Me," Wisdom interjected. *"I did not call you to preach about Me; I called you to be a voice that I could speak through. As you abide in Me and My words abide in you, you will bear fruit that will remain. By My word, the creation was brought forth, and by My word the new creation will come forth in you and in My people. My words are Spirit and Life. My words give Life. You are not called to just teach about Me, but to let Me teach through you. As you dwell in My presence, your words will be My words, and they will have power."*

I thought of something that Margaret Browning had once said: "Every bush is aflame with the fire of God, but only those who see take off their shoes. The rest just pick the berries."

"Lord, I want to see you in everything," I said.

"I will give My messengers the vision to see My purpose in all things," He responded. *"I will make My messengers flames of fire such as I appeared at the burning bush. My fire will rest upon them, but they will not be consumed by it. Then mankind will marvel at*

this great sight and turn aside to see it. I will speak from the midst of My messengers, calling My people to their destiny and to rise up as the deliverers that I have called them to be."

I then felt drawn to the door. I stepped closer to it and could see writing. I had never seen writing like this before. It was of the purest gold, and somehow it was alive. I began to read.

For by Him all things were created, in the heavens and on earth, visible and invisible, whether thrones or dominions or rulers or authorities—all things have been created by Him and for Him.

And He is before all things, and in Him all things hold together.

He is also head of the body, the church; and He is the beginning, the first-born from the dead; so that He Himself might come to have first place in everything.

For it was the Father's good pleasure for all the fulness to dwell in Him,

and through Him to reconcile all things to Himself, having made peace through the blood of His cross; through Him, whether things on earth or things in heaven.

And although you were formerly alienated and hostile in mind, engaged in evil deeds,

yet He has now reconciled you in His fleshly body through death, in order to present you before Him holy and blameless and beyond reproach—

if indeed you continue in the faith firmly established and steadfast, and not moved away from the hope of the gospel that you have heard, which was proclaimed in all creation under heaven, and of which I, Paul, was made a minister.

Now I rejoice in my sufferings for your sake, and in my flesh I do my share on behalf of His body, which is the church, in filling up that which is lacking in Christ's afflictions.

Of this church I was made a minister according to the stewardship from God bestowed on me for your benefit, that I might fully carry out the word of God,

that is the mystery which has been hidden from the past ages and generations; but has now been manifested to His saints,

to whom God willed to make known what is the riches of the glory of this mystery among the Gentiles, which is Christ in you, the hope of glory.

And we proclaim Him, admonishing every man and teaching every man with all wisdom, that we may present every man complete in Christ.

And for this purpose also I labor, striving according to His power, which mightily works within me (Colossians 1:16-29).

As I read these words, they were like a transfusion of life. A single word from God is worth more than all of the treasure on earth! I thought, How could I ever allow myself to be so carried away with the cares of the world when I have His words? I began to think about how worthwhile it would be to cross the earth to hear just one anointed sermon, but sometimes I was so lazy that I did not want to drive across town. I was appalled at my carelessness with His Word as I stood before the door. "Lord, I am so sorry," I blurted out.

As I said this, the door opened. As it did, I pondered how it had looked so dull and uninviting from a distance, but up close it was more intricate and beautiful than any door I had ever seen. That is how people judge the church, I thought, and how I have often judged it myself. I have loved God for a long time, but failed to love His people the way that I should.

"Such repentance will open the door for you to go forth into the purpose for which I called you. You cannot fulfill your purpose apart from My people. I have called My people to be one, and now it will come to pass. Apart from them, you cannot live what you have seen in your visions. Now you must go from seeing the way and knowing the truth to being a vessel for My life. This you cannot do apart from My people. The Father has given you His love for Me, that His love might be in you, just as I asked. Now I will give you My love for

My people. My messengers must see them as I do and love them as I do. As you truly love My word, the door to your destiny with My people will open for you."

His words did not just touch my mind, but also my heart. I felt each one. Just hearing the love with which He spoke of His people imparted that love to me. This was a greater love than I had ever felt before, but it was also familiar and I had experienced it to a degree when I had heard anointed preaching. I thought about how in my foolishness, I had often said that there would be no preaching in heaven, but now I felt that it could not be heaven without preaching. I began to even crave the preaching of His word.

"Yes there will be preaching and teaching in heaven. For all of eternity, My story will be told. That is why it is called the eternal gospel. I am the Word and I am Truth, and words of truth will forever fill My creation. All of creation will delight in My words of truth just as you are now. Even the angels love to listen to your testimonies, and they will hear them. My redeemed ones will forever love to tell and listen to the stories of My redemption. But now you must tell them to those who dwell in darkness. The word of your testimony will liberate many. Those who love Me love My word. They love to read it and they love to hear it. You have been given the truth that will set men free, which is My word in your heart. Go forth with My word. Go forth and you will see the power of My word."

CHAPTER XIII

the manna

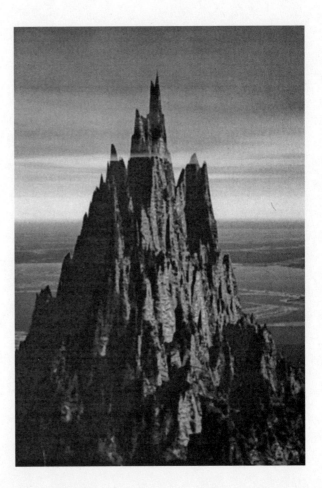

I stepped through the door. When I did, I was surprised that all of the glory in which I had been standing before was gone. It was dark and musty, like an old cellar. It was disconcerting, but I still felt the power of the words that the Lord had spoken to me, and they steadied me.

"What you feel is the anointing of the Holy Spirit," a voice said from the darkness.

"Who are you?" I asked.

"Must you ask?" It did not quite sound like Wisdom, but some other familiar voice. Even so, I knew that it was Him. Gradually, my eyes adjusted to the darkness and I was surprised to see my old friend, the white eagle.

"He lives in you, and so you can abide in all that you just experienced here just as you did in His presence there. I know that you have become addicted to His presence, and this is right, but here you must learn to recognize Him in many forms. First you must recognize His voice in your own heart and then as He speaks through others.

"This you have known before, and have experienced from time to time, but not like you must know it now. He will never be far from you and can always be found easily. He will always lead you to the truth. Only by the Holy Spirit can you see and know anything or anyone the way they really are. In the times that are before us, we will perish if we do not follow Him closely."

"I know that this is true because I hear Wisdom speaking through you. Are you here to show me the way? I can hardly see here."

"I will come to you from time to time to tell you about the signposts that will let you know that you are still on the right path, but the Holy Spirit must lead you. I will also help you to understand how He leads you in different places, but first I must tell you about the manna so that you can live."

"Manna! Do you mean like the manna that Israel ate in the wilderness? Is that what we eat here?"

"It is what all who have walked with God have lived on since the beginning. The manna that Israel ate while in the wilderness was a prophecy of this. The Lord will give you fresh manna daily. Just as He covered the earth with manna every day for Israel while they were in the wilderness, He covers the earth each day with truth for His people. Every way that you turn, you will see it. Even in the midst of the darkness and gloom, His Word will surround you, and you can gather it. Those who are cast into the inner prisons will awake to find it every day. Those who live in great palaces can also find it every day. But His manna is as gentle and light as the dew, and easily trampled. You must be gentle and light of heart to see it."

Living Epistles

"The Lord speaks every day to each one of His people. They cannot live by bread alone, but must have the words that proceed from His mouth. These are not the words that He spoke in the past, but the words that He speaks to them each day," the eagle continued.

"Many are weak because they do not know how to gather the manna that the Lord gives to them each day. They go astray because they do not know His voice. His sheep know His voice, and they follow Him because they recognize it. The manna is the bread of life that each of His people is given each day. You must learn to recognize it, and help His people to recognize this manna. When they taste it as you are tasting it now, they will diligently search for it each day. Do not be concerned about hoarding food or water, but learn to see and partake of the manna that He gives daily. This will preserve you when all else fails.

"The Scriptures are the meat that the Lord gives to us, but His manna is found in His living epistles, His people. He will speak to you each day through His people. You must open your heart to the way that He is found in His people if you are to partake of the heavenly manna. Just as He said to Jerusalem, He is saying to us, "You shall not see Me until you say, 'Blessed is He who comes in the name of the Lord!'" This spoke of Him when He walked the earth then, and it speaks of the way that He is walking the earth now through His people. As our love for manna grows, so will our love for each other. If you are growing in love, the manna which He serves will never taste old or stale to you, but will be new each morning.

"His manna may come to you through the words of a close friend or one of His people who lived long before you as you ponder their writings. He will also speak through those who do not know Him, but you will know that He sent them to you. You will discern His manna when you go beyond just trying to hear His words and seek to hear the Word, Himself. It is not just hearing His words, but hearing His voice that will lead you in the way in which you are to go. Many repeat the words that He has spoken, but His manna is the word that He is speaking now.

"We need the strong meat of the Scriptures to build ourselves up and give us the container for gathering His manna. Grow strong on the meat of His written Word, but also develop a taste for His manna. The meat of His written Word will build us up and prepare us for what is to come, but manna will sustain us through what lies ahead.

"The words that were spoken to you through the saints in the Hall of Judgment were manna from Him. His people are also His manna to the world. Manna is the bread of life— the living words which He speaks to His people daily and are spoken through His people. The Scriptures are set and cannot be changed. They are the anchor for our souls. However, the Book of Life is still being written. He writes a new chapter in the Book of Life with each soul that comes to Him."

Victory or Defeat

"The Scriptures are the blueprint for His dwelling place that He is building among men. They are the testimony of the way that He has worked through men and women to bring about their redemption. His people are the vessels of His living word and are witnesses to the world that His words are not just history, but are still alive and still give life. If you are to know His words, you must know both the Scripture *and* His manna. The Scriptures are His eternal plans that will not change which we must know to walk in His ways. His manna will give you the strength to walk each day. This is so that we might have fellowship. 'If we walk in the light as He Himself is in the light, we have fellowship with one another,'" the eagle said.

"Many of His messengers do not even know that they are being used in this way. They often do not know when He is speaking through them. Those to whom He is speaking seldom recognize His voice. This must change. His people are called to be in unity with Him in all that He does, but few even know His voice. Therefore they seldom follow Him in the way that He wants to lead them. He now wants all of His people to know when He is speaking through them or to them. Just as the sure communication between a general and his soldiers can determine the outcome of the battle, the strength of His communication with His people will determine their victory or defeat in the days to come.

"He is now preparing many messengers who will go forth with His messages. They will also teach His people to know His voice and to know His ways. You must receive His messengers as if you are receiving the Lord, Himself. You must help them along their way. The success of their ministry will determine the rise and fall of many."

For a moment I thought that if the Lord was sending them, surely they would not need my help. This brought a stern rebuke from the eagle, who could also discern my thoughts.

"Do not think that way! Many of His people fall because of that delusion! He could do all things without us, but He has chosen to do them through us. We are His provision for one another. He sent the Helper to live in His people;

188

therefore, He intends for His people to receive their help through one another. Do not ever forget this. That is why He gives us our manna through one another. He has designed all things so that we must love Him above all things, but we must also love one another. We need Him above all things, but we also need each other. In this way, we are also kept humble so that He might trust us with His grace and power."

"I'm sorry," I replied. "I know all of that very well, but I tend to forget it at times."

"The times that you have forgotten this have been more costly than you need to know at this time, but to forget this in the future will be more costly than you can bear. We need the Lord above all, but we also need all of His people. It is in His people that we will find the Helper, the One who leads us into all truth and the One who leads us to the Son.

"He is now sending forth His messengers. Some will be old and wise. Others will be young and have little experience, but they will know His voice. The enemy will also be sending his messengers to sow confusion. This, too, is a part of our training. Some will be deceived by the messengers of the enemy for a while, and others will suffer loss because of them, but those who love the Lord and His truth will not be deceived by them for long. Those who love Him and His truth will know the truth. Those who have been deceived for a time will learn from this, and they will be used to expose the deceivers in the days to come.

"Some who have been the most deceived in the past will become some of the strongest in the truth because of their wisdom. Wisdom is to know His voice and to follow Him. These will not be easily distracted from Him again. Do not judge others because of their past, but by who they have become. Those who have followed Wisdom will have their weaknesses turned into strengths. No one is stronger or more trustworthy than those who know His voice and follow Him.

"We must not stop encouraging His people to know His voice. We must charge His prophets to confront and expose the false prophets. This message we must carry to the end. We are being sent to help build His lines of communication with those who will be His soldiers in the great battle to come. *All* of His people must know His voice. The time will soon be upon us when all who do not know His voice will be deceived by the darkness. Those who know His voice because they know Him will not be deceived."

As the eagle spoke, his words continued to wash me just as they had when they came in the presence of Wisdom. I could not see Him, but I knew that He was present and that He was the One speaking to me. Though I could not see as much with my eyes in this place, I had great clarity of mind that enabled me to understand. I had always felt that I had a very poor memory, but although He now was saying much more than He ever had before, it seemed like I could remember every word He said, even when it came through someone else. I then knew that this was the power of the Holy Spirit Who brings all things to our remembrance. In Him, looking backward or forward was no different from looking at the present. As I was thinking about this, the eagle continued.

"This place seems musty and old because very little fresh air has been let in here for a long time. You have found the door and have entered. The same door that led you to this place also can now lead you back to the Hall of Judgment. What did you receive in the Hall of Judgment?"

"Wisdom and understanding," I replied.

"In a single word, you received grace," the eagle responded. "The Throne of Judgment is also the Throne of Grace. You can boldly go there at any time."

When he said this, I turned to see the door behind me. Now I could see beauty in it that was even greater than when I entered the Hall of Judgment. I opened it and stepped through again.

CHAPTER XIV

the call

I looked at Wisdom, who then turned me around so that I could behold the Great Hall again. I was startled to see standing right behind me everyone whom I had previously met there. I was even more surprised by how much more glorious they now seemed.

"They have not changed," Wisdom said. *"You have changed. Your eyes are opened to see more than you could before. The more clearly that you are able to see Me, the more you will be able to see Me in others."*

I looked toward the Apostle Paul. He was regal beyond description. He had such great authority and dignity, but was at the same time so graced with humility that I am sure the lowest peasant or sinner would have felt completely comfortable approaching him. The desire to be just like that flooded me.

I then looked at the others and felt as if they were all the closest family and friends I had ever known. It is impossible to describe how I loved them and how I knew that they loved me. No fellowship on earth could compare, but the best on earth was somehow a foretaste of this. There was no pretension, posturing or positioning. Everyone knew everyone else completely, and love was the source of every thought. Eternity with this family was going to be even better than I had ever imagined. I desperately wanted to take all of them with me, but I knew that they could not leave their present domain.

Wisdom again answered my thoughts, *"They will be with you as I am with you. Remember, they are the great cloud of witnesses. Even when you do not see them, they are as close to you as they are now. All who have served Me from the beginning are one body and they, too, will be with you in what is to come, but I will be in you."*

I wondered how anything that we experienced in eternity could be better than what was to be found right here in the Judgment Hall. The judgment came from every thought being made manifest. It was not a judgment of punishment, but liberation, if there was no attempt to hide anything. Freedom came with everything that was illuminated so that there was a desire for every heart flaw to be exposed. The love was so great that I knew everything would be covered and made right.

"Everything that you feel in My presence is true," Wisdom continued. *"This love and closeness that you experience here with your brethren are real. You are all one in Me, and you will grow in this love as you grow in Me. As you do, this same love will help others to enter the freedom you have experienced here. When My people who now walk the earth embrace My true judgment, they will walk in a freedom that will enable Me to touch the world with My love.*

"It is not My desire that any should perish or suffer loss when they come here. I desire for all to judge themselves so that I will not have to judge them. That is why My judgments are about to come to the earth. They are coming in ever increasing waves, so that the world may believe and repent. Each trumpet sound will be louder than the previous one. It is the job of My messengers to help the world understand the sound of the trumpets.

"Remember that those with whom you must walk on earth are also members of My body. They have not yet been glorified, but you must see them as they are called to be, not as they appear now. You must love them and see the authority and grace in them that you now see in these. Remember that those with whom you walk on earth now see you as you see them. You must learn not to see according to their present appearance, but see who they are to become.

"Only those who live by My judgments and abide with Me as their wisdom can see My authority in others. Even so, do not strive to have men see My authority in you. Do not be concerned by whether others see you as you are; only be concerned about recognizing others as they are and seeing Me in them. When you become concerned about how others see you, you lose your authority. When authority becomes your goal, you will begin to lose true authority. You know the ministry and authority that I have given to you; do not ask people to call you by your position, but by your name. Then I will make your name greater than your position.

"In My kingdom, authority comes from who you are, not your title. Your ministry is your function, not your rank. Here rank is earned by humility, service and love. The deacon who loves more is higher than the apostle who loves less. On earth, prophets may be used to shake the nations, but here they will be known by their love. This is also your call—to love with My love and serve with My heart. Then we will be one."

CHAPTER XV

worship in spirit

As I listened to Wisdom, it was difficult to comprehend anyone, even this great cloud of witnesses, desiring authority or position in His presence. It seemed that in every moment I had spent here, He had become greater in glory and authority, and I knew that my vision of Him was still limited. Just as the universe was obviously expanding at a great pace and the vastness of it was already incomprehensible, our revelation of Him would likewise be expanding for eternity. "How could mere humans ever represent You?" I questioned.

"When My Father moves His little finger, the whole universe trembles. To shake the nations with your words does not impress anyone who dwells here. But when even the least of My brethren on earth shows love, it brings joy to My Father's heart. When even the most humble church sings to My Father with true love in their hearts, He silences all of heaven to listen to them. He knows that one cannot help but to worship when they are beholding His glory here, but

when those who are living in such darkness and difficulty sing with true hearts to Him, it touches Him more than all of the myriads of heaven can.

"Many times, the broken notes from earth caused all of heaven to weep with joy as they beheld My Father being touched. A few holy ones struggling to express their adoration for Him has many times caused Him to weep. Every time I see My brethren touch Him with true worship, it makes the pain and grief I knew on the cross seem like a small price to pay. Nothing brings Me more joy than when you worship My Father. I went to the cross so that you could worship Him through Me. It is in this worship that you, the Father and I are all one."

Of all that I had yet experienced, the emotion coming from the Lord as He told me this was greater than I had ever experienced. He was not weeping or laughing. His voice was steady, but what He was telling me about worship came from such depths within Him that it was almost more than I could take. I knew that I was hearing the deepest love of the Son of God—to see His Father's joy. True worship from the embattled, struggling, believers on earth could do this like nothing else could.

For the first time, I now badly wanted to leave that place, even with all of its glory, just to get into even the most dreary little worship service on earth. I was overwhelmed by the fact that we could actually touch the Father. One person who worshiped Him from earth during these dark times meant more to the Father than the millions and millions who worshiped Him in heaven. From earth we could touch His heart at this time like we might never be able to do again! I was so overtaken by this that I did not even realize I had fallen prostrate. I then fell into something like a deep sleep.

I saw the Father. Millions and millions were attending Him. His glory was so great and the power of His presence so awesome that I felt that the whole earth would not have even measured as a grain of sand before Him. When I had once heard His audible voice, I felt like an atom standing before the sun, but when I saw Him, I knew that the sun was like an atom before Him. The galaxies were like curtains around Him. His robe was composed of millions and millions of living stars. *Everything* in His presence was living—His throne, His crown, His scepter. I knew that I could dwell before Him forever and never cease to marvel; there was no higher purpose in the universe than to worship Him.

Then the Father became intent on one thing. All of heaven seemed to stop and watch. He was beholding the cross. The Son's love for His Father which He continued to express through all of the pain and darkness then coming upon Him touched the Father so deeply that He began to quake. When He did, heaven and earth quaked. When the Father closed His eyes, heaven and earth grew dark. The emotion of the

Father was so great that I did not think I could have survived if I had beheld this scene for more than the brief moment that I did.

Then I was in a different place, beholding a worship service in a little church building. As sometimes happens in a prophetic experience, I just seemed to know everything about everyone in the battered little room. All were experiencing severe trials in their lives, but they were not even thinking of them here. They were not praying about their needs. They were all trying to compose songs of thanksgiving to the Lord. They were happy, and their joy was sincere.

I saw heaven, and all of heaven was weeping. I then saw the Father again and knew why heaven was weeping. They were weeping because of the tears in the eyes of the Father. This little group of seemingly beaten down, struggling people had moved God so deeply that He wept. They were not tears of pain, but of joy. When I saw the love that He felt for these few worshipers, I could not contain my own tears.

Nothing I had experienced gripped me more than this scene. Worshiping the Lord on earth was now more desirable to me than dwelling in all of the glory of heaven. I knew that I had been given a message that could help prepare the saints for the battles that remained on earth, but now this did not mean nearly as much to me as trying to convey how we could touch the Father. Genuine adoration expressed by even the most humble believer on earth could cause all of heaven to rejoice, but even more than that, it touches the Father. This is why the angels would rather be given charge over a single believer on the earth than to be given authority over many galaxies of stars.

I saw Jesus standing next to the Father. Beholding the joy of the Father as He watched the little prayer meeting, He turned to me and said, *"This is why I went to the cross. Giving My Father joy for just one moment would have been worth it all. Your worship can cause Him joy every day. Your worship when you are in the midst of difficulties touches Him even more than all of the worship of heaven. Here, where His glory is seen, the angels cannot help but to worship. When you worship without seeing His glory in the midst of your trials, that is worship in Spirit and in truth. The Father seeks such to be His worshipers. Do not waste your trials. Worship the Father, not for what you will receive, but to bring Him joy. You will never be stronger than when you bring Him joy, for the joy of the Lord is your strength."*

CHAPTER XVI

the sin

Then I was standing beside Wisdom again. He did not speak for a long time, but I did not need words. I needed to let what I had just seen saturate my soul. I strove to fathom the great business that we had been given just to be the Father's worshipers. To Him, the sun was like an atom and the galaxies like grains of sand. Yet He listened to our prayers, enjoying us continually as He beheld us, and, I was sure, often grieving for us. He was much bigger than a human mind could ever conceive, but I knew that He was also the most emotional Being in the universe. We could touch God! Every human being had the power to cause Him joy or pain. I had known this theologically, but now I knew it in a way that shattered the seeming importance of everything else.

There was no way I would ever have words to convey this, but I knew that I had to spend what time I was given on earth worshiping Him. It was like a new revelation: I could actually bring God joy! I could bring Jesus joy! I understood what the Lord had meant when He said that this was why He went to the cross. Any sacrifice would be worth it to just touch His heart for the briefest of seconds. I did not want to waste another moment when I knew that it could be spent worshiping Him. It was also obvious that the greater the trials or darkness from which the worship came, the more it touched Him. It made me want to receive trials so that I could worship Him through them.

At the same time, I felt like Job when he said that although he previously had only known Him by the hearing of the ears, when he saw Him, he repented in dust and ashes. I was like Philip who had been with Jesus for so long and did not know that he was seeing the Father through Him. How astonishing our dullness must be to the angels! Then Wisdom spoke again.

"Remember the potential for even the least of My little ones to touch the heart of the Father. That alone makes their value greater than any price. I would have gone to the cross again for a single one of these. I also feel your pain. I know your trials because we share them. I feel the pain and the joy of every soul. That is why I still intercede continually for all of you. There will be a time when all tears are wiped away from every eye. There will be a time when only joy is known again. Until then, pain can be used. Do not waste your trials. Your greatest worship and the greatest expression of your faith that pleases Us will come in the midst of your trials.

"You must see Me in your own heart, and you must see Me in others. You must see Me in the great and in the small. Just as I appeared differently in each of these who now stand before you, I will come to you in different people. I will come to you in different circumstances. Your highest purpose is to recognize Me, to hear My voice, and to follow Me."

As I turned to look at Wisdom, He was not there. I looked all around. I could feel Him everywhere, but could not see Him. I then looked back at the witnesses who stood before me. He was there. I could not see Him, but in a more profound way than I had known before, He was in each of them. As the Reformer began to speak, it was his own voice, but I could hear the voice of Wisdom in him just as when He spoke to me directly.

"He has always been in us. He is in you. He is in those to whom you must return. From time to time, He will appear to you again, but you must know that when you do not see Him as He appears, you can better recognize Him where He dwells—*in* His people. He is Wisdom. He knows how, when, and through whom to speak to you. The ones through whom He speaks to you are a part of the message. Remember what He said when He wept over Jerusalem: 'From now on you shall not see Me until you say, "Blessed is he who comes in the name of the Lord."' You will not see Him unless you can see Him in those whom He sends to you."

"It is easy for me to see and hear Him in you," I replied, "but it is not nearly so easy with those on the earth who have not yet been glorified."

"It is not meant to be easy there," Angelo replied. "To search for Him is the call of the kings who will reign with Him. Those who love Him and who love the truth will search for Him more than they would for the greatest treasures or conquests."

Conquered by Him

"The greatest calling of all is to be fully conquered by Him," a man whom I did not recognize offered, stepping toward the front. "I should know," he added, and then he told me his name. I was shocked that this man would be found in the company of the saints. He had been a great conqueror, but I had always believed that he had done more damage to the name of Christ than possibly anyone else.

"I, too, found the grace of the cross before the end of my time," he said. "You are not just going back to conquer *for* Him, but to be conquered *by* Him. If you will devote yourself to surrendering to Him, He will use you to conquer in His name. True conquest is to capture the hearts of men with the truth that sets them free. Those who follow Him more closely will be used to conquer the most and will be the greatest of kings. On the earth, these will seldom realize that they have conquered anything. They will not see what they have really accomplished until they get here. Those who lay up great treasures on earth—even treasures that may be considered spiritual—will have little here."

"On earth you cannot measure eternal treasures," Paul said. "When I died, it looked like everything for which I had given my life to building on earth had already perished. The churches I had given my life to raising up were falling into apostasy, and even some of my closest friends were turning against me. During my last days, I felt that I had been a failure."

"Yes, but even I count Paul as a spiritual father," the great conqueror continued, "as do most of us who are here. Most who will come through the great battle of the end will be victorious because he was faithful to stand for truth. You will not measure true spiritual fruit rightly while you are on the earth. You can only measure your true success by how much more clearly you are able to behold the Lord, by how much better you know His voice, and by how much more you love the brethren."

Then Paul spoke again.

"For months before my execution, I did feel like a failure. However, on the day of my execution I was reminded of Stephen who I had watched die at my own feet years before. The memory of the light that was on his face that day had carried me through many trials. I always felt that he had somehow died for me so that I could see the true light. I knew that if I died like Stephen, then even if everything else I had done had been futile, it would insure that my life would not have been in vain. I was so thankful that I really was dying for the sake of the gospel, even if it did not look then like my ministry had accomplished very much.

"As the revelation of this came upon me, so did the grace, and my last day on earth was the most wonderful of all. I then realized that as I had lived and sincerely tried to die daily to my own desires in order to serve the gospel, every time I denied myself, there were eternal seeds planted even though I could not yet see them in the temporary realm. Being here, I can now see that this is certainly true. You must not try to judge by the fruit you see on earth, but do what you must do because it is right.

"Even so, more than bearing fruit, your call must be to know the Lord. If you seek Him, you will always find Him. He is always near to those who draw near. Many want His presence, but they do not draw near. You must do more than *want* Him: You must *seek* Him. This is part of your call. There is no higher purpose. Your victory will be measured by your seeking. You will always be as close to Him as you want to be. Your victory in life will be according to your desire for Him."

Then Paul lifted his hand and pointed to me. "You have been given much, and much will be required of you. Even if you bury many of the talents entrusted to you, you can accomplish far more than others, but you will have failed in your commission. You must never measure yourself by others, but keep pressing forward, seeking more of Him. And yet, with all of the glory that will be revealed to you, never take off that cloak!"

Sowing and Reaping

I looked down at the cloak of humility to which he was pointing. In all of the glory that I was now seeing, its drabness seemed multiplied. I was appalled that I looked so bad standing in their presence. I drew it back to see the armor under it, which was now more brilliant than I had seen it before. It was so brilliant that the more I uncovered it, the more the group in front of me faded because of its brightness. However, I was feeling far less embarrassed with the brightness of my armor shining out. I then decided to take the cloak all of the way off while I was there so that I would at least not feel as repulsive in the presence of so much glory.

There was silence, and I stood quietly for a few moments. I was unable to see anything because of the brightness of my own armor. I did not understand why I could not hear anything either. I then called out for Wisdom.

"Put your cloak back on," I heard Him reply. I did as He said and began to dimly see the outline of the Great Hall again.

"Lord, what happened to everyone? Why is everything so dim again?"

"You can see nothing here without wearing that cloak."

"But I have it on now, and I still cannot see very well," I protested, feeling a terrible desperation.

"Every time you take off humility you will be blinded to the true light, and it will take time for you to be able to see it again."

Even though I was beginning to see the glory again, it was nothing like before. My vision was coming back, but very, very slowly. I was grieved beyond words.

"Where is Paul?" I asked. "I know that he was about to tell me something very important."

"When you took off your cloak, all of those who were here departed."

"Why? Why would they depart just because I took off the cloak? I was just embarrassed by my appearance. Did that offend them?"

"No, they were not offended. They knew that you could not see or hear Me through them without the cloak, so they returned to their places."

I was more grieved than ever at this statement. "Lord, I know that what they were about to say to me was very important. Will they return?"

"It is true that you missed an important revelation by taking off your cloak. It would have helped you, but if you learn the lesson not to ever take off the cloak again, especially for the reason that you just did, you will have learned another important lesson."

"Lord, I think that I have learned that lesson. I do not remember ever feeling this bad. Can they not come back now and share what they had for me?" I begged.

"All Truth and all Wisdom comes from Me. I speak through people because the people I speak through are a part of the message. While you remained humble enough to keep your cloak on, I could speak to you in glory. Whenever you take off that cloak, you become spiritually blind and deaf. I will always speak to you if you call on Me, but I must change the way that I speak to you.

"I do not do this to punish you, but to help you receive your vision back more quickly. I will give you the message that I was going to give you through these witnesses, but it must now be given through your enemies. It will come with trials, and you will have to bow very low to receive it. This is the only way that you will get your vision back as quickly as you will need it. For what is coming, you must be able to see."

Brokenness

The grief I felt was almost unbearable. I knew that what I could have received in such a glorious way was now going to come through great trials, but even worse than that was the

217

fact that the great glory which I had beheld just a few minutes before was now so dim.

"Lord, I am sorry for what I did. I now know how wrong it was. The pain of this mistake is almost too much to bear. Is there no way that I can just be forgiven and receive my vision back? It does not seem right that one brief moment of pride should be this devastating," I pleaded.

"You are forgiven. Nothing is being done to you for punishment. I paid the price for this sin and all others. You live by My grace. This is not because of the Law of righteousness. It is because of My grace that there are consequences for sin. You must reap what you sow or I could not trust you with My authority. When Satan took his first step into self-seeking and pride, multitudes of My angels who I had entrusted to his authority followed him. When Adam fell, multitudes would suffer. For those to whom I give such authority, there is a corresponding responsibility. There can be no true authority without responsibility. Responsibility does mean that others will suffer if you go astray. Mistakes have consequences.

"The more authority you are given, the more that you can either help or hurt others by your actions. To remove the consequences of your actions would be to remove true authority. You are a part of the new creation that is much higher than the first creation. Those who are called to rule with Me are given the greatest responsibility of all. They are called to a position higher than Satan held. He was a great angel, but he was not a son. You are called to be a joint heir

with Me. Your whole life, both the trials and the revelations, are all for the purpose of teaching you the responsibility of authority.

"For every lesson that you must learn, there is an easy way or a more difficult way. You can humble yourself, fall on the rock and be broken, or the rock will fall on you and crush you into powder. Either way, the final result will be brokenness, which is humility. Pride caused the first fall from grace, and it has caused most of the falls since. Pride always results in tragedy, darkness and suffering. It is for your sake and for those whom you are called to serve by having authority over that I will not compromise the discipline you must learn by reaping what you sow.

"Adonijah boasted that his father, King David, did not discipline him. Solomon complained that he could not get away with anything without his father's discipline. Although Solomon thought that he was not being treated fairly, David was not being unfair. He knew that Solomon was called to be a king. Those who receive the most discipline are those who are called to walk in greater authority.

"You were blinded because you stepped out of humility and began to move in pride. The humble cannot be embarrassed. When you start to feel embarrassed, it is because you are beginning to move in pride. Let the embarrassment be a warning that you have departed from wisdom. Never let embarrassment control your actions. If it does, you will fall even further. Learn to embrace every opportunity

to be humbled, knowing that I will then be able to trust you with more authority.

"Do not boast in your strengths, but in your weaknesses. If you will openly talk more about your failures in order to help others, I will be able to more openly display your victories, 'For everyone who exalts himself shall be humbled, and he who humbles himself shall be exalted.'"

I knew that everything He said was true. I had preached the same message many times. I thought of how Paul had warned Timothy to pay attention to his own teaching and realized that I felt that I needed my messages more than those to whom I preached. Now I was more ashamed by the shining armor I wore than of the humble cloak. I pulled the cloak even tighter. When I did this, my eyes brightened and my vision grew strikingly better, even though it was still far from what it had been.

I turned to see the door. I was afraid to go back through it, at least until I had received more of my vision back.

"You must go now," Wisdom said.

"What is on the other side?" I asked.

"Your destiny," He replied.

I knew that I must go. I was still very sorry that I could not enter the door again with the vision that I had previously because I already knew how dark it was on the other side. I will be even more dependent on others for a time, I thought and committed myself to trusting the Lord and not my own vision. Immediately my eyes grew brighter again. I started to look once more back at the Great Hall to see if they were as bright as they had been, but decided not to. I just determined that it was better now not to look back. Then Wisdom appeared beside me, almost as brilliant as before. My eyes had adjusted to the light so quickly that I could now look at Him. He said nothing, but just looking at Him gave me great courage. Even so, I still felt remorse that I had not heard all of the message I had been about to receive from the cloud of witnesses.

"If remorse is turned into resolve, the trial will be much easier. Then when your enemies appear to exalt themselves over you, you will grow even more in the authority to prevail over My enemies."

When I looked back at the door, I was amazed. I saw so much more on it now than I had seen before that for a moment I thought that I was at a different door. It seemed to have grown still more beautiful and was unlike any door I had ever seen, even in this realm. There were exalted titles written in a most beautiful script, all in gold and silver. There were beautiful jewels I did not recognize, but that were so compelling it was difficult to turn my gaze from them. They were all alive. I then realized that the entire door was alive.

As I gazed at the door, Wisdom laid His hand on my shoulder. *"This is the door to My house."* When He said this, I immediately understood that the attraction I now felt for this door was the same that I felt when I looked at Him. It *was* Him somehow. How could anything this beautiful have looked so plain and uninviting before, I pondered. The Lord answered my unspoken question.

"You cannot see My house as it is until you see Me in My people. As you began to really hear Me through My people just before you took off your cloak, your eyes were opened to begin seeing My house as it is. There is much more glory to be seen in it than you can now behold. This is the door, but there is much more. When you return to the realm of your own time, this is what you must seek. This is what you must lead My people to. This is what you must fight for, and this is what you must help to build—My house."

With Wisdom's hand upon me, I walked toward the door. It did not open, but I passed right through the midst of it. I do not believe that there is a human language that could describe what I felt as I passed through. I saw the glory of all ages in a single moment. I saw the earth and the heavens as one. I saw myriads of angels, and I saw myriads of people who were more glorious than any angel I had yet seen. These were all serving in His house.

Now I knew the call. Even though I had already been through so much, I knew that my quest was just beginning.

About the Author

Rick Joyner is the founder and executive director of MorningStar Publications and Ministries in Charlotte, North Carolina. He has written more than a dozen books, including *Shadows of Things to Come, A Prophetic Vision for the Twenty-first Century, The Prophetic Ministry, The Harvest,* and *There Were Two Trees in the Garden.*

Rick is also the editor of *The MorningStar Journal* and *The MorningStar Prophetic Bulletin,* and is the director of the MorningStar Fellowship of Ministries and the MorningStar Fellowship of Churches.

Rick lives in North Carolina with his wife, Julie, and their five children. Rick can be contacted by writing MorningStar Publications, 4803 West U.S. Highway 421, Wilkesboro, NC 28697 or by fax at (336) 973-5191. MorningStar's Web site is located at www.morningstarministries.org.

Other Titles by Rick Joyner

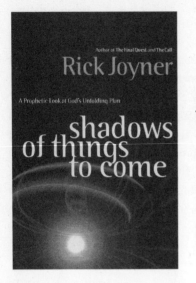

Shadows of Things to Come

A Prophetic Look at God's Unfolding Plan

"One of the greatest sources of prophetic vision is found by better understanding our past," says Rick Joyner. "I studied Christ's interaction with the apostles, as well as the life of the early church, to be obedient to a heavenly vision in which I was told that I would not be able to accurately foresee the future until I understood the past."

In this important book, Rick Joyner looks at the life and ministry of the apostles and of later generations of believers so that Christians today can close the openings the enemy has used to gain entry and do his deadly work.

ISBN 0-7852-6784-0 ✦ Trade Paper ✦ 240 pages

A Prophetic Vision for the 21st Century

A Spiritual Map to Help You Navigate into the Future

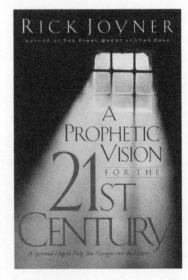

A Prophetic Vision for the 21st Century is a vision of the future. It is also a call, a manual, and a strategy for mobilizing the most powerful army that has ever marched upon the earth—the army of God.

This book is a call for Christians, who have been privileged to live in possibly the greatest times of all, to arise and fulfill their destiny. It is a manual for how we can use the divinely powerful weapons we have been given to confront the great darkness that is now sweeping the earth. It is also a strategy for how we can begin to demonstrate the power of the kingdom that is coming.

Will you answer the call to be a part of God's kingdom, and to stand for truth, righteousness, and the liberation of the world, which our King purchased with His own blood? This is the greatest call of all—and it is your call.

ISBN 0-7852-6936-3 ✦ Trade Paper ✦ 264 pages